DRIVEN

UNDERSTANDING AND HARNESSING
THE GENETIC GIFTS SHARED BY ENTREPRENEURS,
NAVY SEALS, PRO ATHLETES, AND MAYBE <u>YOU</u>

DRIVEN

DOUGLAS BRACKMANN, PhD.,
AND
RANDY KELLEY, MBA

LIONCREST
PUBLISHING

DRIVEN

*Understanding and Harnessing the Genetic Gifts Shared by
Entrepreneurs, Navy SEALs, Pro Athletes, and Maybe You*

ISBN   978-1-61961-693-6 *Paperback*
       978-1-61961-694-3 *Ebook*

First, above all, praise and thanks to the Creator and Sustainer, who made me such a driven explorer! To my brothers in and from the "Teams," thank you for your brotherly love, the fire in your guts, and your totally incorrect sick senses of humor. You all are the wolf pack of wolf packs (skip to Chapter 11 for you reading-challenged). To my family, friends and fellow entrepreneurs, thank you. We are not at all "self-made," but "community-made," and you've been an incredible community. To the Driven, accept your weirdness, love it, create, create, create...and play!

This is for my family who has learned to embrace my Driven nature and has taught me to love myself through all my own self-judgment. This is for the thousands of clients who have taught me everything I know and have witnessed my growth as well as their own. This is for all the Driven who don't know how to accept their different natures so that they may be freed from shame. And finally, this is for the Great Mystery of a thousand names that we all may share in abundant Grace.

CONTENTS

"*A master in the art of living draws no sharp distinction between his work and his play; his labor and his leisure; his mind and his body; his education and his recreation; he hardly knows which is which. He simply pursues his vision of excellence through whatever he is doing, and leaves others to determine whether he is working or playing. To himself, he always appears to be doing both.*"

—FRANCOIS AUGUSTE RENE CHATEAUBRIAND

· CHAPTER 1 ·

THE GIFT OF DIFFERENCE

"I have always been driven to buck the system, to innovate, to take things beyond where they've been."
—SAM WALTON

The year was 1908. A bright young man named Napoleon dropped out of law school. Finances had been a problem for him from the time he was born, and he lacked the financial means to continue. After a brief attempt at law school, he took a job as a reporter. One day, he got an assignment that would change his life—and the culture of America—forever.

Napoleon's assignment was to interview Andrew Carnegie, one of the most powerful men in the world. Carnegie, a poor Scottish immigrant who had accumulated a massive fortune of over $300 billion, decided to teach the young Napoleon the secrets to success. Napoleon Hill, as you know him, used what he learned from Carnegie in his book *Think and Grow Rich*. It became the most popular self-help book ever written, with sales of over 70 million copies.

People crave wealth; they want to be successful. A book promising to reveal these secrets is irresistible, especially if the secrets are something anyone can learn. Hill's book has sold hope for decades. The first couple of chapters preach the importance of ambition and resolve. Phrases like "burning desire," "consuming obsession," and "bulldog determination" fill the pages. Threaded throughout are countless stories of successful men with an unwavering sense of purpose.

Such lessons have persisted across the decades. Tony Robbins's seminars teach us that "the path to success is to take massive, determined action." The magic of determination is communicated even in marketing. Nike commercials urge us to "Just Do It." These messages endure because they appeal to the dreamers and the wannabes.

Stories of Henry Ford, Thomas Edison, and Charles

Schwab will inspire almost anyone, but inspiration is very different from action. The reality is, not everyone *can* do it. If everyone had it in them to do it, we would all be rich, powerful, and, in the world's eyes, successful.

This internal fire that we have seen in people like Elon Musk, Bill Gates, and Steve Jobs cannot be taught. It does not come with a new belief or a new way of looking at a problem. It is inherited and then fed with the right environment and course of action. It can be honed, sharpened, and developed, but this drive is something you're born with.

Nearly 10 percent of the population possesses a genetic difference that, with the right environmental conditions, manifests in a powerful, unstoppable drive. This drive is the difference between dreaming and doing. The Driven, those who possess this genetic variation, differ on many neurobiological attributes. If you are Driven, you are different from most of the people in your life.

The Driven can do what others cannot. We (both authors included in this group) can juggle twenty different variables in our heads at a time; we notice things other people miss; we have the resilience to withstand challenges that others give up on. We crave adventure and risk. We want something new, something more, something better. Our genetic difference has been evolutionary gold for society. It has enabled humanity to survive when the world was a very harsh place, when society depended on the talents and abilities of the Driven for their existence.

When the Driven are lucky enough to fall into the right environment—an environment in which our particular abilities are a fit—we become superheroes. We are multi-million-dollar entrepreneurs, Olympic and pro athletes, Navy SEALs, and first responders. While the safe but predictable monotony of a 9 to 5 and W-2 paycheck is usually not for us, we can excel in business—usually in sales, development, and anything dealing with innovation. We need that risk, that uncertainty, and that danger in our lives.

If you are Driven, you come equipped with the biological wiring to succeed, whether in a multinational corporation or doing surveillance work in a foreign country. Your drive is a powerful engine that can take you anywhere. If, however, you do not fall into that ideal environment and are unaware of your gift, or let it run unmanaged, your life may be fraught with internal misery and chaos.

A gift, however, no matter how extraordinary, can cause a fair amount of trouble for you if you don't know how to use it. Do you remember the 1980s sitcom, *The Greatest*

American Hero? In the show, schoolteacher Ralph Hanley encounters some aliens who present him with a very special superhero suit. When he wears the suit, he's imbued with fantastical powers. He can fly, has remarkable strength, can become invisible, and has a host of other incredible abilities.

The trouble is, Ralph loses the instruction manual. He has no idea how the suit works, and he must learn by trial and error. He gets into the suit and flies around, but he flies horribly and crashes into buildings. He doesn't know how to control his X-ray vision. His mishaps lead invariably to some disappointing, though admittedly amusing, consequences. Those watching Ralph who don't know his circumstance might conclude that his special suit is broken or defective in some way. But, in truth, Ralph has mismanaged the gift he's been given.

Sometimes we have gifts we aren't sure how to use, gifts we don't really understand. These gifts come with some pretty amazing abilities if we know how to use them. Without the instruction manual—in other words, if we haven't learned to harness these powers—we often seem different or broken, not only to others, but to ourselves.

If you are one of the world's roughly 10 percent possessing the genetic alleles and life experiences that manifest this powerful drive, the right instruction manual will catapult you to a life beyond your wildest dreams. If you *don't* know how to use this drive, it can cause havoc. Your genetic difference can lead you to feel there is something wrong with you, and the associated shame can create a hellish existence. It may even kill you. This is the dark side of drive.

You may be intimately aware of this darkness. You may have experienced it through a tragic life circumstance, trauma, or midlife crisis. The Driven are at risk for addictions they believe will provide relief. The remaining few who are not lost to life-sabotaging addictions may end up accumulating much of the world's wealth, but may damage their bodies. Most of us will struggle to maintain a balanced life as we tend to push hard at whatever we become driven towards.

Who are the Driven? We're the kids and adults who seem to be continually distracted; we often can't concentrate on a TV show we haven't chosen, yet we immerse ourselves so deeply into a personal interest we seem to be in another world. We're the folks with addictive personalities (you find many of us in Alcoholics Anonymous). We are risk-takers. We're perfectionists and yet we're never satisfied. We're the people who are perpetually questing for something new—new job, new home, new spouse, and new technique to improve our world—because we're sure the grass is greener on the other side. We're brilliant problem-solvers, miss nothing going on around us, and can learn super-fast, but often come up with poor grades in school. We may have companies worth millions, then somehow manage to risk it all—and may even wind up bankrupt multiple times throughout life.

Some of the population looks at people like us and thinks that we may have a disorder. Since their discovery around thirty years ago, these genetic and neurobiological differences—which can manifest as the world's greatest innovators, star athletes, and heroes—have been vilified and pathologized. We're diagnosed with ADD or ADHD. We're told we have depression or OCD or other anxiety disorders, that there is something wrong with us, that we have "special needs." We may even believe we are mentally ill.

We Driven often fall into self-destructive addictions, which are then presented as proof that we are "disordered." We are not disordered. Rather, those of us who possess this genetic difference have the biology for extraordinary drive. Our brains and bodies are wired differently, and this difference is a great gift to both us and mankind.

Sadly, in our society, behaviors that deviate too greatly

from the norm are deemed dysfunctional and in need of treatment. After all, if you can't focus in class, if you're never completely satisfied in any job, if—despite an all-consuming obsession to learn—you lose all interest once you master a skill, then something must be wrong with you. You must be broken if you prefer to endure a root canal rather than sit for hours at a quiet dinner with the in-laws. It can't be normal to be able to have the TV on and have your eyes on your iPhone while your wife is talking to you, but when she goes off in a huff, you can recite word-for-word what she said. There must be a diagnosis that explains these behaviors. And there must be a medication to treat it.

This may or may not sound familiar, depending on whether you were graced with the right environment that capitalized on your Driven traits. Either way, you may suspect that you are different.

Western medicine and modern science have not done a very good job of understanding this difference. Anything different in society is viewed with suspicion or caution. With the technological revolution over the last fifty years blasting what is considered "normal" into our living rooms with increasing speed and color, the social scripting for what is acceptable has taken shape on a global scale. We fear what we do not understand. We demonize that which does not fit in. Worse, we use what we do not understand today as a weapon against those who exhibit behavior outside the norm.

The bulk of the studies on people with ADD/ADHD stem from the foundational belief that "these poor patients with this affliction must be cured." This has created research designs that don't really tell us what we want to know. ADD/ADHD has been defined simply by a list of behavior traits. When groups are compared, the differentiating criteria are behavioral, rather than revealing the underlying causes for the behavior. When those diagnosed with ADD/ADHD are compared to those deemed normal, it is not exactly clear what causes the differences. All we learn from such studies is that there *are* differences. Without an understanding of the reasons and their evolutionary benefits, it's easy to consider them defects.

Thanks to recent scientific advances in the ability to explore our neurobiology, we are beginning to understand the potential genetic and environmental underpinnings of these differences. Many of the traits presented here have long been considered maladaptive; but they, in fact, have an invaluable evolutionary ability to survive in a *much more dangerous world*.

People may have told you that you need medication to

function, that you are destined to have a tough life. These people couldn't be more wrong. The only thing they are right about is that you are different. Fortunately, different is good.

Far from being a disorder, what is being medicated is actually an evolutionary advantage under conditions that challenge survival. This advantage, when understood, results in an incredible set of gifts to both you and mankind. All you need is the instruction manual.

WHY WE ARE DRIVEN: EVOLUTIONARY CLUES

A potential evolutionary explanation for ADD/ADHD behavior first drew attention about thirty years ago. Psychotherapist, entrepreneur, and talk radio show host, Thom Hartmann (you may recall his talk show *Big Picture* on the Russia Today cable network) posed a new model for understanding ADD/ADHD. According to Hartmann, the traits associated with ADD/ADHD wiring are the results of an evolutionary adaptation intended to protect the species. People with these traits possess what he termed a hunter's brain—a brain equipped with abilities to help them survive in a pre-agrarian society.

Before the agricultural revolution, the hunter's skills and abilities were highly valued and necessary for survival.

The agricultural revolution marked the shift toward a much safer farmer's world. Centuries of environmental influence resulted in the evolution of a farmer's brain suited to a very different set of survival requirements. The hunter's traits and abilities, which were once an advantage, were increasingly mismatched with society's new needs.

Initially, Hartmann's theory was met with skepticism and rejection, especially from the community of scientists, drug companies, and mental health professionals who were making a fortune manufacturing and distributing drugs to treat the condition. They deemed his work soft science and pop psychology.

Since his original theory was proposed, and the publication of his follow-up book, *The Edison Gene,* along with breakthroughs in science and technology—specifically, the mapping of the human genome and the incredible advances in MRIs of the brain—many have found great support for what Hartmann proposed. A global study that mapped genes across our species compared the genomes of a traditional hunting culture to that of a traditional farming tribe and found genetic differences—specifically, twenty-three statistically significant differences in the DNA. (Hartmann recently received an apology from the psychiatric community for their initial hostile rejection of the model.)

WIRED FOR DANGER IN A SAFER WORLD

Evolutionary change is based on the need for adaption. We adapt because there is good reason for it, because that adaption will help ensure survival. Human beings have a very different relationship with the environment than the rest of the flora and fauna on this planet. The slow but steady adaptation of genetic natural selection is the norm, but not for humans.

All other animal and plant species are bound by the "survival of the genetically fittest" system, which keeps the pace of change between competitive species in check. There is natural genetic variance in traits and skills across all species. All cheetahs run fast, but some are really fast. All gazelles run fast, but some add increased speed and agility to the equation. Over time, as the faster cheetahs eat the slower and less agile gazelles, only the faster, better-equipped animals are left to pass on their genetics. Species adapt slowly together. Neither species changes faster than the other species adapts. The slow-paced, genetically-adapted change in predator and prey results in the same relative level of danger over multiple generations of the species.

The human neocortex came along and broke this natural balance between species. We have a massive brain that allows us to consciously learn to master the environment at a faster rate than our genetics, or the genetics of those we share this planet with, can adapt to. This advantage has allowed us to be a dominant force in the animal kingdom. All the species around us never had a chance. The wooly mammoth is extinct because we invented the spear. Because of our ability to learn, we ate many species faster than they could genetically adapt to the new threat we posed to them.

Although we have made the world safer through our abilities, our inventions, our innovations, and the other artifacts arising from our superior brain, we are all genetically wired for a world that did not include these changes—for a more dangerous world, a world that no longer exists because we made it safer. Simply put, our genetics have not yet adapted to the changes that we have deliberately made to our environment. Though some of us have acclimated to this safer world, we are all still essentially a fear-based animal in a world that is relatively safe.

Why have some of us retained our Driven gifts, while others have been able to acclimate to that 9 to 5 job as accountants, teachers, and managers? Is it nature, or is it nurture that influences behavior? The answer is simply "yes." No longer can these two influences be considered separate, nor should they be.

The field of epigenetics (the study of the interaction of genetics and environment) demonstrates that adaptive genes may turn on and off depending on environmental conditions, but this is often on a generational time scale—and usually not overnight. While every human on this planet has the exact same set of DNA, changes to the expressions and interactions of this DNA with the environment have made every human unique in their genetics.

The Driven seem to be a normal variant of both gene expression and brain structure, who have better adapted to live in a world that is more dangerous than those who have become acclimated to the safer agricultural world that now exists. Why these Driven adaptations are so persistent can only be speculated.

We do know that being exposed to a dangerous world seems to lead to becoming more biologically prepared for long-term stress for several generations to come. This means that even if you did not have a tough childhood and your parents did not either, the genes to prepare you for adversity may have been triggered in previous generations. Multigenerational studies demonstrate differences in psychobiological traits in holocaust survivors. Rachel Yehuda's research in epigenetics of the children of holocaust survivors has found biological adaptations in the offspring for as many as four generations, and counting.

Yet research explaining why some family members in the same home and exposed to the same stress demonstrate very different physical, psychological, and biological reactions is not conclusive. Though the field of epigenetics is growing at an exponential pace, the more we uncover, the more we recognize how little we actually understand about the ridiculously complex interactions between nature and nurture.

The purpose of this book is not to make scientific inquiry into these interactions. Rather, the goal is to inform the reader that these behavior patterns are a normal variant of human behavior. The Driven are not broken. They possess exceptional gifts. When you understand this, you can move beyond the social stigma and personal shame often associated with these differences. More importantly, you will be able to follow the Mastery Path, the lifelong path toward learning to use the powerful advantages you, as a Driven person, possess. As someone who is Driven, you are uniquely suited to the Mastery Path. On the Mastery Path, you will learn to harness your gifts and thrive even if the world does not seem a fit for you.

THE GIFT OF A BACKWARD BRAIN

We've seen that Driven people have retained the gifts that allowed them to survive in the harsh, pre-agrarian world. Much evidence supports their psychobiological differences. ADD/ADHD meta-analysis research affirms that those diagnosed with ADD/ADHD (when compared to control groups) rely on different areas of the brain to make sense of the world. These findings, the results of hundreds of studies with many thousands of participants, may explain the differences between the behaviors of the Driven and the controls. The neurostructural differences in the Driven translate to a markedly different set of skills and abilities.

The brain has four different areas that are each associated with different functions—the frontal, parietal, temporal, and occipital lobes. The frontal lobe is responsible for executive functions—reasoning, planning, problem-solving, and thinking. The parietal lobe is associated with perception of stimuli—pressure, temperature, and pain. The temporal lobe is concerned with auditory stimuli and memory. The occipital lobe is associated with visual stimuli.

The frontal lobe is generally considered the chief executive of the brain. One of its main functions is to determine the most important thing to focus on right now, in the way a CEO determines what a company's main focus is. It then tunes out things that are off target and not as important to survival.

The Driven brain seems to work differently from the non-Driven with respect to functional dominance. Non-Driven people have frontal lobe dominance. Think of your accountant, patiently focusing on the figures before her, or your son's third grade teacher, correcting his essay.

Compared to those acclimated to this safer world, the Driven have hypofrontality, meaning an underactive frontal lobe (this is one of the defining features of ADD/ADHD) and greater occipital dominance; in general, the Driven rely more heavily on the occipital lobe (which is at the back of the brain) to navigate the world. They depend primarily on visual cues or stimuli to make sense of their landscape. They see first, and think second. In the pre-agrarian, dangerous world in which split-second reactions could mean the difference between capturing prey and going hungry, or becoming the victim of a predator, occipital dominance and hypofrontality were an advantage. Hypervigilance of our environment and using our eyes kept us alive.

Because Driven people primarily use the back of the brain to navigate the world, our frontal lobe is open to more information and is able to consider multiple variables at the same time. This type of brain has the ability to multi-think, considering multiple, seemingly unrelated concepts simultaneously. It seems those wired for a less-safe world can detect and visually track multiple threats or opportunities and keep track of them all at the same time. To be clear, this is not the same thing as multitasking. Nobody can multitask. It is actually only possible to do one thing at a time.

The computer is a great metaphor for the ability to multi-think. The hypofrontal Driven brain is like an operating system that is able to run a number of different applications at one time. If you have the ability to multi-think, even though you are concentrating on one of the applications, the others are still working in the background. Background programs pop up when a relationship between the programs comes to our minds. The Driven can see unique connections between these multiple concepts. We can then come up with new associations and solutions to problems that the normal brain can only dream of. We are uniquely creative in this way.

When we attempt to explain the tangents and connections between seemingly unrelated topics to a non-Driven person, they look at us as if we are crazy. The big picture created by all these seemingly unrelated variables makes sense to us; it was critical to us all those eons ago. Farmers tending to crops and livestock required (and still require) a different set of skills; they could not get sidetracked chasing butterflies or coming up with new ideas on how to pump water—if they did, their survival would be jeopardized.

Most Driven people report that their mind is considering dozens of variables at the same time with rapid speed and skill. Apple and Microsoft executive and author Linda Stone terms this phenomenon Continuous Partial Attention (CPA). The Driven are especially skilled at this on a neurostructural level. We put the "hyper" in hypervigilant. This ability is one of our greatest gifts and potentially one of our greatest problems.

Every one of the thoughts in our frontal lobe potentially carries with it a small-to-large emotional charge. Each of these can stack on each other and ramp up sympathetic arousal. The Driven can experience extreme sensory overload. This may explain, in part, why Driven people rely on the sympathetic branch of our central nervous system (CNS) as a primary means of going through the world. We keep our foot on the gas pedal, which creates incredible drive, but can wear out the parts of our machine much faster.

Envision our example of having multiple computer applications working at the same time. Now, imagine that each of these applications has a sound component—music, sound tones, or a voice speaking. You may be concentrating on one of those applications, but you can hear the sounds from those other applications at the same time. You become distracted as your brain tries to filter them out and concentrate solely on what you were intending to work on. Even if you try to tune these other sounds out, eventually they overwhelm your senses. Juggling multiple variables and connecting seemingly unrelated ideas are not without consequences—and those consequences can tear our lives and our bodies apart.

No wonder the Driven are prone to anxiety and to addictions in an attempt to cope. This may partly explain why some of us love nicotine and other stimulants, whether they are one of the heavily prescribed ADD/ADHD medications or even just the little kick we get from Sudafed or a strong cup of coffee. These drugs help speed up the underactive frontal lobe and can give us more clarity of thought. They help us concentrate on what is in front of us and filter out all those other thoughts that are trying to permeate our consciousness. We find that our brains work better on these substances, and many of us just don't want to give them up, despite the risks.

We are not suggesting anyone get off medications. If they work for you and your body tolerates them well, you are lucky. If you are on medications, you should never stop them all at once, and only make a change after you've talked at length with your prescribing doctor. Regardless of whether you are taking medications, this book will help harness your powers and perhaps enable you to live in a way you never dreamed possible.

THE GIFT OF ALLELES DRD2-A1 AND DRD4-7R

How do we know when we are heading in the right direction and have successfully completed a task to our satisfaction? We feel rewarded. Our feeling of being rewarded is biologically directed, triggered by the neurotransmitter dopamine, a chemical that fits like a key into a receptor on a nerve cell causing it to fire.

When enough neurotransmitters fit into enough receptors on a particular nerve, the nerve fires and releases neurotransmitters that trigger the next nerve to fire. This causes a cascade of neural firing that creates sensations recognized by the individual as a reward. All of this happens in nanoseconds. This process requires that a sufficient number of neurotransmitter keys open enough receptor locks to make a neuron fire. If there are not enough keys, then nothing happens.

Neurobiological research supports that the Driven differ genetically in the way their reward systems function. For reasons only speculated, about 8–15 percent of the population have an allele, or mutation that changes the number of receptors on the D2/D4 receptor sites, as well as the way dopamine is transported between the cells to these reward centers in the brain. These alleles impact the way the D2 and D4 reward centers fire, causing them not to fire as easily. The Driven may possess one or both of the allele genes DRD2-A1 and DRD4-7R. If this is the case, then no matter what we do, we don't feel rewarded, at least compared to those who do not have these genetic alleles.

The implication of not feeling fully rewarded in our lives is far-reaching and can have profound consequences. Because of the Driven's deficiencies in feeling rewarded, we are likely to perpetually seek dopamine, constantly questing to have our reward system activated. If we believe that the dopamine we crave will eventually come, we may drive ourselves into the ground trying for it, persevering well beyond what any normal person would tolerate. The Driven are innately pulled toward the success they believe will finally leave them feeling rewarded. Whether we are trying for the thousandth time to create a light bulb, ride a massive wave, climb a mountain, train and complete an Ironman, or even withstand the tortures of the Navy SEAL BUD/S training, we don't quit. We may die trying. The unending quest to feel rewarded drives us through incredibly difficult circumstances.

We must be very careful with the attributions we assign to not feeling rewarded. If we attribute feelings of not being rewarded to something within ourselves, a potentially immutable characteristic, we create a self-concept as inadequate, unworthy, and a failure. We can start a downward spiral into limited self-worth and despair. Changing the attributions, you connect with the sensations you experience, as someone with D2/D4 can empower you to use your Driven gifts and free yourself of shame forever.

There are, of course, individual differences across those of us with Driven-type alleles. When a gene is expressed, it is not going to be expressed in the same way for everyone. You may have a lot of a certain trait expression, while another person with the same gene only has a little of that gene's expression. Additionally, nerves are adaptive, and they change based on environmental conditions. Even if you have these genes, how much it takes for you to be rewarded will be different than everyone else on the planet, even if they are also D2/D4. A person may have the genetics for shyness, but life experience certainly influences those genetic tendencies. However, the point of this book is not to explore the influence of genes on behavior; rather, it is to refine the way you operate in this world.

THE GIFT OF SPIDEY-SENSE

Driven people are said to have Spidey-Sense, in reference to the superhero Spider Man's ability of uncanny intuitive powers. We tend to know something almost immediately and may not be sure how we know it. This Spidey Sense was an important factor in survival. Historically, hunting in groups, we needed the ability to sense where other hunters were. As we waited out of sight from each other when the woolly mammoth or other threatening predator approached, we needed this extra sense to keep us alive. We had to rely on each other, both in hunting and escaping from threat. When one of the herd sensed a threat, there had to be some means of communicating this threat rapidly and silently amongst the members. We had to be able to instinctively know what the pack intended, to have an extrasensory means of communication.

If we were to make any noise, or worse—shout out, or make obvious signals with our hands—the saber-toothed cat could quickly note our position or the herd of deer we spotted could be alerted to our presence. We needed the ability to stay still when scared or when getting ready to pounce on game, prepared for the threat or the opportunity. The Driven's ability to sense danger or good fortune with our gut instincts helped ensure our survival.

Fast-forward to the twenty-first century. The Driven's

supernatural sense of intuition and gut instinct make them human BS-detectors. This can be a huge advantage but, like many of our skills, also a curse. For instance, when someone says you look good today, or that they like your new haircut, your gut may tell you they are just saying it to charm you or sway your opinion. We may question everyone's motives, even to the point of seeming paranoid. This can create huge issues for those around us, and lead to difficulty in trusting anyone, even in our closest relationships.

Of course, this intuition is a gift if you are a salesman and can sense when you're losing a customer. It's a gift when you can tell that the stock market is ripe for a shift. It's a gift if you are going into harm's way, and your gut instincts turn up your alert level. It's a gift that can save lives.

SUPERMAN: ALONE AT THE TOP

Few people are comfortable alone. Humans are social creatures. These social orientations served a critical function in the survival of the species. Early man lived in groups as a way of staying alive. These initial tribes gave way to complex societies. Although current technology-based needs draw more heavily on the skills of the farmer than the Driven, the social needs that were initially hard-wired into humanity remain.

Fear of being cast out of the human herd is one of the most powerful psychological forces in our human experience. We seek refuge within social groups. Although a Driven may not fit into a farmer's world, we, like all social animals, need the community and companionship of group affiliation. Fear of being exposed as "odd" or "abnormal" is a strong motivator for many of the Driven to disguise themselves as someone without these gifts. It is human nature to want to be accepted.

Real acceptance is hard to come by when you lead exciting lives the rest of the human herd can only dream of living. The majority of people do not live thrilling lives. They sit on a couch watching the Driven on TV. To most people, we are superheroes; those without our gifts, idolize us. This can further contribute to the feelings of isolation and alienation we often experience. We may feel like we're unusual, but we want to be accepted so that we aren't alone. Thus, we hide our gifts.

Consider Superman. He is "faster than a speeding bullet, more powerful than a locomotive, able to leap tall buildings in a single bound." The problem is, there is only one Superman—alone. His secret home is, after all, called the Fortress of Solitude. Nobody, not even Superman, wants to be lonely. Thus, he puts away his cape and superpowers, and puts on glasses, so he can belong. Under the guise of bumbling Clark Kent, he can have friends. He suppresses his superpowers in order to be perceived as no one special, as no different from the rest. In fact, he goes to extremes presenting himself as a "mild-mannered" reporter, an introvert that would not hurt a fly. If someone strikes him, he does not punch him into the next county; he turns the other cheek. He does everything he can to maintain the "normal" persona, donning the cape and tights only when he feels driven to use his super abilities.

For most of the Driven, this disguise has detrimental consequences. When we masquerade as someone else, suppressing our natural self, we may feel like a phony. This is popularly termed the imposter syndrome, when people pretend themselves into a persona and perpetually feel like a sham or charlatan. Moreover, for all our achievements, we never feel like we are truly successful. Even though we may have the money, house, car, degrees, titles, trophies, or a life that looks shiny and pretty on the outside, still we may not feel rewarded on the inside. As we have shared, it is much more difficult for you as a Driven to feel rewarded than it is for the non-Driven.

Regardless of what you do, whether it's winning a coveted award or running a marathon, you feel it isn't enough because you haven't felt your reward; and, because you don't feel your rewards, you assume you haven't yet earned them. People look at our success and tend to think we have no problems. It is actually quite the opposite. Being Driven can lead to great success, but this success may come at a very high price, both physically and socially.

The Driven who do not have the instructional manual for their gifts are at risk for a variety of negative consequences if they try to force their Driven orientation into the modern, safe world's landscape. We hide, in a sense, hoping that no one discovers our deeper, darker, flawed "self"—who we feel we are inside and then confirm it's looking back at us in the mirror. We may have a deep, dark shame that there is something missing or wrong with us. We may get stuck in "if only" thinking, sometimes driving ourselves to great accomplishment, believing if we only had X or achieved Y, then we would be okay. These very feelings may be the ones that drive us to attempts at perfection or glory. Underneath, we may feel that no one really knows what it is to be like us, with the underlying feelings of being different and not good enough.

This genetic wiring sustained us when the world was much harder to survive in. From the perspective of those acclimated to the safer agrarian world, with two years' worth of grain stored, there is nothing to be worried about. As the Driven, we still have that fear in us that it is not enough. There is never enough. We are not wired to survive in this safer world; we are wired to survive in a world that created a constant challenge. Thus, we often make our world harder, which looks like over-achievement to everyone else, but to us, feels like not enough.

Innate gifts and talents aren't always obvious or easy to develop or easy to navigate. We may struggle with them, much like Superman did; or, like the Greatest American Hero, we may fumble about as we learn to use them, crashing into a few walls in the process. The rest of the population has a brain and reward system designed for the safe agrarian world they created, and so they are likely to understand and explain typical Driven behaviors as a problem. It certainly can be a problem from their perspective. But, as we have shared, these traits and behaviors are not evidence of a defect or a disorder. Rather, they are simply the outcomes of misalignment of the Driven's brain and biology with the modern environment designed by those most acclimated to it.

Once those of us with these Driven traits can re-conceptualize our purpose so that it maps to our genetic blueprint and begins to harness our latent potential, we can be excellent at what we do in the world as it is now. Again, we are not broken; the world around us is designed by those different from us, and we forgot, over time and over generations, what our purpose in society was.

It was a collection of Driven brains that put a man on the moon and created the iPhone. It is the Driven who can take an idea and create a company that will dominate in the market within months or years. We are Driven. All that energy, which is not very useful when a class of children learning their ABCs is channeled into a force that cannot be stopped when leveraged correctly. These individuals become super-charged with purpose and focus. The Driven can see problems miles away. They can sense things others do not perceive; they can tell what others are feeling and thinking. This is no psychic trick; it is because they have an awareness that others do not. It is exactly that awareness that kept our Driven ancestors safe at night and allowed an awareness of where their prey was hiding in the tall grass.

The Driven are more likely to take risks, calculate a multitude of adjustments at the same time, and can change direction with lightning speed. The hunter, for example, needs to be able to change course quickly when hunting prey. He has to be able to make a decision in a split second or he will miss opportunities. The problem is, when this ability is not properly channeled, these gifts may end up being used in ways that sabotage us. If we cannot work with them, they can ultimately control us and become obstacles to the life we want.

Imagine what you could do in your life if you could channel

your energy, lightning fast decision-making abilities, and focus into a business or idea. If you look at some of the greatest innovators and most successful people in business, you'll find many of them, at one time in their lives, were labeled ADD/ADHD, or at least had the majority of the symptoms associated with the diagnosis. When we know how to use our gifts, we're in good company. Albert Einstein, Galileo, Mozart, Leonardo da Vinci, Charles Schwab, Walt Disney, John Lennon, Greg Louganis, Winston Churchill, Henry Ford, Stephen Hawking, Jules Verne, Alexander Graham Bell, Woodrow Wilson, Hans Christian Andersen, Nelson Rockefeller, Thomas Edison, Gen. George S. Patton, Agatha Christie, John F. Kennedy, Henry David Thoreau, David H. Murdock, Dustin Hoffman, Pete Rose, Russell White, Jason Kidd, Russell Varian, Robin Williams, Louis Pasteur, Wernher von Braun, Dwight D. Eisenhower, Robert F. Kennedy, Prince Charles, Gen. Westmoreland, Eddie Rickenbacker, Gregory Boyington, Harry Belafonte, F. Scott Fitzgerald, Mariel Hemingway, George C. Scott, George Bernard Shaw, Beethoven, Carl Lewis, "Magic" Johnson, John Corcoran, and Steve Jobs all share our characteristics.

· CHAPTER 2 ·

IDENTIFYING YOUR INTERNAL EXPERIENCE
THE BIOLOGY BEHIND THE PSYCHOLOGY

"Everything we hear is an opinion, not a fact.
Everything we see is a perspective, not the truth."

—MARCUS AURELIUS

Envision this scenario: Doug has a coffee mug in his office. The handle is obviously on one side. If he places this mug on his desk so the handle is not facing the client, from the client's perspective, the mug has no handle. If for some reason the client doesn't like cups without handles, he's going to have all kinds of feelings and beliefs about this cup. If he thinks Doug would give him a cup without a handle, he's going to be angry with Doug.

The client believes that the cup has no handle because he believes what he sees; his confidence in the reliability of his perceptions coupled with his feelings about cups without handles can block any curiosity about alternative perspectives. If he won't question his perceptions, the cup will remain objectionable, and anyone even considering handing him such a cup knowing his feelings about handle-less cups is, at the very least, a jerk.

These perceptive biases permeate everything we see. You've probably gone to the movies with a friend and the two of you have come away with two very different interpretations of the characters' motivations, or even the point of the story. In a classic example of the power of perception, twenty-five people may witness a car accident, but every one of those people will tell an alternate version of the accident; they all have a different internal experience of this same accident depending on their history, their beliefs about cars, and where they were standing when the accident occurred. It is through our internal experience that we interpret the actual or real world.

Often there is a disconnect, as in the case of the cup, between that real world (the external reality) and what our internal experience of that reality is. Humans are not really living in reality. We are living in a bias of what we see is happening, think is happening, and what we feel is happening, rather than what is actually happening. Our neurobiology and neural structures prevent us from seeing the world as it actually is. As a result, we all develop an internal world that differs from the external or real world.

We draw on our most available or accessible experiences when we make sense of the world. If as a child, a dog bit you, as an adult, you may see dogs as dangerous animals. The friendly Labrador Retriever across the street may make you uneasy. Your internal experience in this case is colored by the history you have with dogs. It has created an internal world that differs from the external one.

These perceptive biases are perpetual yet constantly adjusting to your current state of being. Say you buy a yellow car. All of a sudden, you see yellow cars all over the road. You buy a pair of tennis shoes. Two days before you bought them, you never saw anyone wearing that particular brand of shoes, but the moment you buy them, it seems everyone's wearing them. You think, "Wow, they're everywhere!" The tennis shoes are meaningful to your inner experience, so they become a more prominent feature of the outer world. In reality, the number of people wearing tennis shoes and the number of yellow cars most likely have not changed at all.

Roughly 10 percent of the information about our world taken in through our senses is deemed relevant enough for our reticular activating system to pass it along into the higher regions of our conscious brain. When you dine in a crowded restaurant, there are conversations all around, but you tune them out as you talk to your companion. It is only if you hear your own name, something relevant to you, that you instantly tune in to the voices around you. If you like red cars, you're more likely to notice red cars. If you witness a car accident between a red and blue car, you will not attend as closely to the blue car; your focus will be on the red car. This bias, or set of expectations, results in our focusing on what is important to us, and ultimately what we perceive. And we literally don't see or experience the outer world or reality. All of this is automatic, subconscious, and common to everyone on this planet.

People's perceptions can become their reality—an unquestioned internal experience. What we perceive is essentially governed by how we interpret reality, and our internal reality creates our perspectives, a tunnel, through which we view the world. If this sounds circular, you're right. It is. We are subconsciously biased in perceptions that confirm our biased perceptions. We all live, to varying degrees, blind to our ego tunnel—limited by what our subconscious brain deems worthy to pass along to our conscious brain.

How to see past our biases into the real world is a question that philosophers have pondered throughout the ages. Until we gain insight, we are unable to see outside of this internal experience. The challenge and skill of stepping out of our internal experience is an incredibly powerful tool for creating a new world for us. This tool is critical for developing and sustaining relationships.

Literally, a relationship is the ability to see outside of our own internal experience so that we can relate to what the other person's perception is. The word relationship means we have an agreement. We agree that my perception is different than yours *about the same reality*. I can relate to what your perception is from your inner-world perspective, and I invite you over to my inner-world perspective.

If you understand that the person across from you can't see the handle on a cup because of his view of the cup, his reactions will make sense to you and you'll be able to address his concerns. This "emotional" intelligence is dependent on the ability to take the other's perspective. Without that understanding, the conversation may become adversarial. Without the needed perspective-taking, neither party can empathize. This inability to take perspective creates friction between all of us, but can really escalate between the Driven and the rest of the human race.

An understanding of how our internal experiences function is especially important to those with Driven genetics and brain structures. If the Driven are locked inside of this fear-based ego tunnel, they may never get a reality check. If we feel unrewarded and we attribute those feelings to something wanting within ourselves, an inability to see outside of our internal experience dooms us to continue feeling that way. Our different interpretation of the world can create a break in communication and a chasm in relationships. If we are completely locked into our internal experience, we have little hope of understanding why others disagree with us. Our relationships are likely to suffer, or possibly, not exist at all.

No two people have an identical internal experience, even when they have grown up together or share many of the same experiences. The unique way we encode experiences and perceive the world is not controlled solely by experience. The interaction of our experience and our own genetic blueprint crafts our internal experience. Understanding this interaction is critical to harnessing our Driven gifts.

THE DIVIDED SELVES: MONKEYS AND ELEPHANTS

Questioning of the self is not new. Since man first painted himself on the wall of his cave, this primitive self-reflection served some role in making sense of life.

An early metaphor for the *self* depicts human behavior as being directed from two seemingly different sources. This three-thousand-year-old metaphor explaining our behavior can be observed as if we are an Indian elephant in a wrestling match, vying for control, with a bunch of monkeys sitting on its shoulders trying to direct its behavior with elephant hooks. With their poking and nudging, the monkeys seem to be able to get the elephant to obey most of the time; at other times, the elephant seems to have a mind of its own, ignores the monkeys, and does what it wants.

Little did these early psychologists observing human behavior know how scientifically spot-on they were. The monkeys are our conscious brain. They can reason; they consciously know what they want the elephant to do. With a little nudge and coaxing, the body will do what our consciousness wants us to do. The elephant is the subconscious reptilian brain and the rest of our body; just as you don't have to consciously think to pull your hand away from a hot stove, the elephant also just acts without thinking or direction from the monkeys.

The elephant can drive your car and go on autopilot, while your logical monkeys are dreaming of pizza and looking for a good song on the radio. They are remarkably independent and free to act completely self-sufficiently. However, at times they are in perfect sync. This concept is explored in greater detail later in the book, but for now, consider this simple question:

Which one are you: The elephant or the monkeys?

This is a trick question. Many, when asked this question, answer one or the other. Some think for another minute, and then say both, which is more accurate. But the answer that will help you move ahead in mastering your gifts is, "both and neither."

A response of "neither" indicates a curious non-judging consciousness that can set us free from the chattering of the overly rational monkeys and the impulsiveness of the stubborn elephant that doesn't care about future consequences. Being able to stop and observe the mental chatter and feel the beginning impulses of the body—*and not act on either*—is the logical container that is required to change.

A logical container "contains" you and your experience and frees you from the judgment that ultimately undermines you. It's logical because it holds the logical truth that what we see, feel, experience is through a biased biological wiring system. It is a place to be able to observe without making quick judgments.

The logical container empowers you to be able to see the world through the curious eyes of a newborn. Through our curiosity, we can begin to see the world with less bias, and not the world distorted by our lens of pre-existing experience, values, and judgments which, for the Driven, will include a fair amount of fear and discontent.

BUILDING THE LOGICAL CONTAINER TO HALT THE PERSONAL NARRATIVE

The process of building a logical container requires that we accept a few simple truths. Whatever religious beliefs we place faith in, it is undeniable that we are animals (and God's creatures, if you choose to believe). To be able to build the logical container, you must accept that you are an animal with a common biology that drives you; you must accept that you have perceptions that may hide reality from you. The logical container allows for the simple understanding that our perceptions are not reality, and that both conscious and subconscious forces drive our behavior.

We are neither the personal narrative nor the

self-judgments created in our heads. We are not the opinion-laden story of ourselves, nor are we the emotions connected to our perceptions. You are not just the monkey mind. Beliefs and emotions are definitely part of us, but the logical container is an acknowledgment that we are much more than just that *and also none of that.* You are not your impulsive reactions leading to poor decisions and outcomes. You are not the mistakes you have made. The logical container will empower you to see outside your perceptual ego tunnel and to look beyond the judgments and expectations you carry. This premise is the factual basis for the logical container that must be created for any and all change to occur in life. Unending curiosity and a basic understanding of your biology will get you started. The results can set you free.

The subconscious is not some mysterious place hidden from our view. It is your body. The subconscious may seem like an independent entity, like an elephant that can be impulsive and "unthinking," but it is not as simple as this. It comprises every cell in your body. Your brain is encapsulated in your skull, but your *mind* is your whole body; it is the brain, but it also contains the interaction of all your cells—the miracle of the central nervous system (CNS).

Like all mammals on this planet, we are wired to live in an almost-constant state of guarding against danger, since we have little control over most things in this world. Unlike the rest of the animals on this planet, we are gifted (or cursed) with a conscious brain and language.

Somewhere in our childhoods, we had the thought, "I am alive." This is the birth of our *neither elephant nor monkeys* self, the birth of our pure consciousness. But soon to follow is the thought, "One day I will no longer be alive." This is the beginning of the limiting conscious, the observing ego of "me" as an individual entity, the one in charge of making sure that the day we die is far into the future. We must trust that this new sense of the "me" is steering us in the right direction, keeping us safe and avoiding harm. This is the *small self*, as it is often termed. This is our personal narrative and often the self that believes they are in charge of the elephant. This is the "me" that believes they are in charge of their own life. But are they? And who is actually doing the steering?

WHO'S REALLY RUNNING THE SHOW?

We have two biological systems running simultaneously, making sense of this experience we call life and keeping us out of harm's way. One, the elephant, is very old; and the other, the monkeys, is fairly new. Both interact frequently but, as discussed, can operate independently. Which one is really in charge—the monkeys or the elephant?

To answer this question, we need to understand our biology. The monkeys are conscious and divided into two categories: rational and abstract. The rational ones keep track of our height, bank balance, weight, education, and the mental models of prediction (if I do A, I can expect B). The abstract ones are mood states creating our emotional self—happy, sad, mad, etc.

Imagine you are in your car driving. The subconscious elephant steers the car and keeps us unknowingly going in the right direction. The conscious monkeys are able to decide which radio station to choose and think about what to have for dinner. These two systems controlling our behavior are happening *at the same time*. But what we are aware of is the logical monkeys recalling what you have in the fridge and what the options are for dinner, while the emotional monkeys are considering what you feel like having for dinner.

Most people go about their day-to-day lives using the conscious brain (the monkey mind) and believing they are in charge of themselves; our conscious mind is responsible for creating a world that suits who we think we are and what we feel we like. Most have the luxury of being unaware of the subconscious system (the elephant) working behind the scenes, steering our lives, or our car, while we are lost in fantasy, worry, or plans for the future.

If this person driving is lost in the sensations and smells of the pizza waiting at home, yet oblivious that they have safely navigated the last few miles, all is right in the world. If a car suddenly swerves into their lane, they are thrown back into their body with a shock, and the thought of warm, delicious pizza is gone. The person immediately turns into an unthinking, reflex-Driven creature. The elephant is completely in charge until the world is safe enough to let the monkeys on its shoulders have control again. This subconscious self and its safety system is why we are still alive, and it has much greater control over how our world looks than previously speculated.

Many people live happily in this internal world of logic and emotion and never have to question who or what they really are. Driven people often lack this luxury. Eventually, our genetics and drive may force us into "self" examination. The trigger for this reflectiveness may be consequences of impulsiveness, addiction, a feeling of being broken, a constant state of fear or guardedness, imposter syndrome, or a change of environment away from one that fits our Driven traits. Our quest for dopamine and our willingness to take risks can create some pretty fun stories, but can also lead to total self-destruction. The Driven, who often suffer from self-sabotaging subconscious impulses—rationalized in a somewhat believable fashion—are often pondering why we did something that seemed like a good idea at the time. We are all a bunch of animals and we may not have as much control over our lives as once believed.

The "mindfulness" movement, that seems to be riding a wave of popularity here in the West over the last forty years, might better be described as a way to recognize the elephant—as a way toward "body-awareness." This also might explain why it is much more popular in theory than practice. To actually be mindful is a lot harder than it seems. Recognizing whatever is happening in the body without judgment, or without trying to manage the elephant, frustrates the monkeys, and we eventually give up on trying to be mindful. It is a great challenge to find and build a strong logical container just to observe the monkey-mind and catch the impulsive elephant before it takes action, but it is a challenge the Driven are up for.

THE SUBCONSCIOUS "ELEPHANT" BIOLOGY: HARDWARE AND SOFTWARE

A basic knowledge of the biology driving our "subconscious elephant" provides insights that can be invaluable in understanding our Driven wiring and in building the logical container we need to take control of our Driven gifts. The older subconscious system running throughout the body comprises a hardware system that "hard wires" experience into the body. The science of this is really cool. If you touch a hot stove, all the cells impacted by this trauma, from the finger all the way to the spine, record this experience as subtle changes to the DNA. All the cells become primed for a repeat of this potential trauma. This cell "memory" helps the cells react to the trauma faster if it happens again, reducing the potential damage. Once the information traveling up the nerve pathway makes it to the spine, an impulse is immediately sent back to contract the muscles and get your finger away from the danger. All the muscles also remember this experience (a phenomenon known as muscle memory), which results in faster reflexes. The body remembers the experience and stores this information. Once we have gone through this reflexive cycle of getting us out of danger, information is passed along up the spine to a slightly newer part of the CNS.

This system can be conceptualized as software. A mental imprint of the senses (sight, smell, touch, etc.) is recorded. In the example of the stove, a mental image of a square metal box with four burners is written into the pattern recognition machine, the reticular activating system. Then the system attaches body sensations to these patterns. The elephant is guided by this software, sending out a subconscious radar, constantly scanning the environment for previously recorded patterns. When a pattern is *close enough* to a previous experience (it doesn't have to be the same stove; it could be simply a glass top with painted burners), the radar is "pinged" and the body is filled with sensations to inform the person that a pattern is matched. The elephant has an impulse to avoid anything that even resembles a stove.

This primitive system is a real-time operating machine, meaning that when we are not asleep, the invisible radar is always on; the elephant is on autopilot and the body is responding reflexively. Most importantly, when no patterns are being matched in the immediate environment (which would be the case only when the immediate surroundings are safe), the system is designed to go into a rest, repair, and restore function. The elephant can relax.

Bodily sensations are simply a constant pinging of the radar. Emotions happen up in the monkey mind, the interpretation of these sensations caused by the pinging. Emotions are a means of telling the animal that *something out there matters somehow to me in here.* The elephant gets a ping of the radar. Almost instantly, sensations in the body are created. This simplistic understanding is needed to build the logical container.

Whether thought or emotion comes first has been a hotly contested question in psychology for over a century. The fMRI has put this argument to rest: the subconscious is actually in charge. The elephant gets the first say in what is happening around us. Feelings or emotions happen *after* the sensations reach the monkey mind. A common saying in the SEAL Teams is a quote from the Greek lyrical poet Archilochus: "We don't rise to the level of our expectations, we fall to the level of our training." The monkeys may do all the planning, but it is really the elephant that carries out the mission.

Mike Tyson's quote says it all: "Everybody has a plan until they get punched in the face." When someone hits you hard in the face, thinking stops and reflexes take charge. If the elephant becomes wild and out of control, you're sure to lose the fight. Thus, the practice of calming the elephant through meditative techniques is critical.

As the elephant calms and conscious awareness is restored, the subconscious seems to quickly and silently slip into the background of our lives until the environment demands it to take over again, or so we believe. As you will learn in subsequent chapters, the elephant really is in charge of most areas of our life, *all the time.* The key to building the logical container is the biological reality that when we are aware of the monkeys chattering, we must be *safe enough* to still be in conscious control of the elephant. The emotion of fear does not exist unless we are safe enough to be aware of it.

THE CONSCIOUS "MONKEY" BIOLOGY: THOUGHT AND EMOTION

If the older (elephant) system is a real-time operating system, the monkey mind (neocortex, or new-brain) is a time machine. This new-brain system is for problem-solving. The elephant addresses problems in this instant in the immediate environment. The monkeys address problems that don't exist right now, but might exist in the immediate-to-distant future—in essence, the monkeys worry (when we are relatively safe and the elephant is not wrestling for control).

The neocortex is separated from the subconscious by the caudate and is designed to work independently from the subconscious most of the time. The level of connection to our body varies. If you're an athlete or into martial arts, you may have amazing embodiment. Most people, however, live in the conscious brain, relying heavily on the left hemisphere of thought and linear logic.

When we first start working with clients, or before our retreats, we send out a link to Jill Bolte-Taylor's TED Talk. Jill suffered from a massive left-hemisphere stroke one morning. Being a neuroscientist, she describes in wonderful color the differences between the linear logical self and the purely abstract and nonlinear emotional self. If you aren't one of the millions who have downloaded and watched this video, it's worth the twenty minutes.

The linear logical and the nonlinear emotional selves can easily be envisioned when you bring to mind your favorite dessert. Try the following exercise. With as much detail as possible, picture your favorite dish. Think about the flavors, colors, and smells, and notice the wonderful sensations of appetite in your body. Now, think about the calories, and think about what this meal may do to your health. Most people will immediately feel deflated from the sense of judgment coming from the left hemisphere.

The battle between the emotional and logical monkeys always brings to mind the classic cartoon with the devil on one shoulder and the angel on the other. These selves seem to be in the midst of a battle; but, for the Driven, the battle may involve whole armies of angels and devils.

THE BACKWARDS BRAIN AND A BUNCH OF MONKEYS

Though multi-thinking is one of the greatest gifts for those that are Driven, for some of us, the multi-thinking becomes neurotic worry that we take to a whole new level. The battle within the Driven brain gets us into non-Driven psychiatric care in a heartbeat, where tons of labels await us.

The Driven often develop obsessive compulsive tendencies trying to manage the monkeys. Some of our clients describe the "layers and layers" of tangential monkeys arguing and trying to come up with a consensus to guide the elephant in what to do next. Some may turn to meditation and other mindful techniques to fight these monkeys, since these approaches are supposed to help us calm down.

Some people report, "Meditation doesn't work for me; in fact, it makes it worse." That may actually be true for the Driven brain. Since we are designed to live in a scarier world, when we drop our guard, our CNS will find another way to cope. Oftentimes, the Driven may "check out" (dissociate) or "go numb" (freeze) when they are asked to focus on their bodily sensation while following the breathing during traditional yoga or meditation practices. It is also important to note that, even if you find these bodily states pleasurable, they are probably taking you farther away from where you want to be. Later in the book, we will discuss the style of meditation specifically designed for the Driven brain and how it can transform your life.

THE RESTLESS GENE: UNDERSTANDING THE IMPACT OF THE DRD2-A1 ALLELE

Metaphorically speaking, the D2's foot is either perpetually on or right above the gas pedal. We're supposed to be ready for action—survival was a 24/7 prospect for early D2/D4s. We needed to survive in a scary world, which required that we be alert to everything. Even today, our inner world of fear keeps us on guard for the next threat or opportunity.

As you have learned, the genetic differences in our receptors result in a lack of dopamine.

Lack of dopamine triggers sensations often perceived as boredom, and these sensations are extremely uncomfortable for a creature programmed to be constantly alert for danger, and not easily able to relax or put on their brakes. An uneventful landscape feels wrong. The elephant is restless, on guard, and raring to go. Our drive for dopamine may result in a variety of risk-taking ventures and interpersonal experiences, which can have terrible consequences.

When first discovered thirty-plus years ago, the DRD2-A1 allele gene was quickly connected to alcoholism and termed the "Alcoholism Gene." It was correlated not only with alcoholism, but also with all types of addictions, from gambling to eating disorders. However, not everyone with this gene had obvious addictions, so it was renamed "Reward Deficiency Syndrome" and attributed to feelings of chronic discontentment and a need for immediate reward.

How does it manifest? Imagine you are watching TV. A small buzzy tension starts in the body. A signal is sent to the problem-solver parts of your brain that you need something—a bag of chips, a different channel, or just to do something different. The elephant squirms and the monkeys chatter away in search of a solution to get away from the unpleasant sensations.

How many times has your spouse or friend criticized you for not being able to just sit down and watch TV? How many times will you flip through radio stations in your car looking for the right song? How often do you get bored in class or at work and you strike up a conversation with the person next to you?

The desire for dopamine and the need to get distracted from the uncomfortable sensations in the body can fuel a desire for mischief-making. D2s enjoy messing with a friend's sense of calm. "Screwing around" is a favorite pastime. You may have been the class clown or the class troublemaker. You are looking for some way to disrupt the boring tranquility that feels so unnatural to you.

D2s are Driven to fix what is wrong right now! We are wired to want something better, so if we notice a problem, we're going to address it. As such, we have a very strong sense of justice. Teaching people "lessons" may be particularly enjoyable. If someone swerves into your lane while you are driving, you may impulsively speed up and give them the rise in their CNS that they just gave you. If somebody makes you feel uncomfortable, you want to return the favor. If someone has wronged you, you feel like you must avenge the transgression.

Unfairness, whether directed at us or others can be intolerable to those that are Driven. What makes us really nuts is to be accused of being in the wrong when we are not, and having no opportunity to explain or defend ourselves. D2s experience a deep sense of unjust shame and actually feel rage at their accuser. The ability to manage the impulse to fix injustice is much harder for D2/D4s than it is for the non-Driven. D2s need to do something about the buzzy tension in their body or it can get overwhelming. Because of our reactions to unfair situations, we are labeled with an impulse disorder, and even considered mean or vengeful. Our need for immediate recourse to resolve the sensations in the elephant is much greater than it is for the other 90 percent of the world. Our determination to get back at whoever has wronged us, or the bully in the office or on the playground, can distance people from us.

Being able to see outside of our internal experience may help us to understand not only another's reaction to our relationship with the world, but can also illuminate for us why we feel and behave as we do. Learning to observe the elephant's sensations before these sensations get the monkey mind going wild is essential. Without this understanding, we may be at a potentially huge disadvantage in navigating the world.

WANDERING GENE: UNDERSTANDING THE IMPACT OF THE DRD4-7R ALLELE

The DRD4-7R Allele, known as the "Wandering Gene," can be traced back to as early as fifty thousand years ago utilizing genetic anthropology. (Cool, isn't it?) *National Geographic Magazine* did a fantastic article exploring these genetics in the January 2013 issue. People with this gene were spread across the globe. A desire to wander to a better place makes sense for those in search of prey. In modern society, we D4s continue running toward the shiny prize that exists off on the horizon. The elephant is always signaling the monkeys that there may be a tree that has better leaves to eat beyond the horizon.

The implications of operating with the D4 reward center, or "Horizoning Gene," as we term it, tend to be much more subtle than in the D2—at least outwardly. If you are primarily a D4, you may have avoided the ADD/ADHD diagnosis altogether (D4s can be quite low on hyperactivity), but you clearly have a Driven brain.

When the D4 reward center is calling for attention, it

creates feelings that the grass is greener over there. "There" could be any place the D4 isn't. This mindset results in the Fear of Missing Out (FOMO). FOMO is a very common concern among both D2s and D4s, but especially the D4 who is chasing dopamine in the future. We're likely to say, "I want to go to that concert because I am afraid of missing out on the fun (missing out on that dopamine)." We're always scared to sit it out.

Future-oriented, the D4s genetics seem to be a driving force in "if only" thinking. If only you had this thing, or achieved that, or became the best in the world at this skill (or at least better than the guy next to you), you would feel the reward and you'd finally feel safe. Every year or two, we get a new job or a new profession. You want to be a teacher at this school. You get there, but then you hear about another school and it's going to be better. You go to that school and you realize that you'd rather be a lawyer. In high school, you wanted to be a doctor one year, a scientist the next, and an airline pilot after that. We are always jumping from thing to thing, from party to party, always looking toward the horizon, primarily because we are searching for that dopamine. We are looking for that reward. The moment we get close enough to it, it loses its shine. We think how great our lives will be once we achieve our objective but, when we get there, it's not that great, and we're off again in search of something better, chasing the next goal, mastering the next skill, or chasing the next thrill.

How many different books are you reading at the same time? How many books do you actually finish? How many books that you've bought do you actually start reading? How many different hobbies do you have strewn throughout your garage? How many seemingly unrelated interests in the next great thing or idea have you had over the years?

Driven to continually try something new, D4s are "Jack of all trades" and masters of many of them. We are the renaissance men and women (think DaVinci), not because we want to be good at all these things, but because we get bored and move onto the next thing.

That said, when we lock onto an interest we may become hyperfocused and tune out everything else. We may or may not return to a previous obsession, but we usually have at least one or more going all the time. Often D4s are seen as having the Type A or addictive personalities. Often, our lives are out of balance.

Our desire for change may extend to the world. We want to make a difference, either just for ourselves or for others. D4s will sometimes be very driven philanthropists.

More competitive than most, we search for rewards through social comparison. Do we play a better game of golf than our buddies? Can we run faster? Are we more successful financially? We also love to wager on almost everything we do with our buddies. This adds the little extra risk we need to get the dopamine pop if we win. This drive to be better than others may have carried you through medical school or to elite levels in a sport or career, but the elephant is never satisfied.

Unfortunately, DRD4-7R can also drive you in the other direction, to self-destruct in an attempt to create the perfect high from thrills or drugs. Riding a twenty-foot wave was great, but just wait and see what I do next! Eventually, the thrill-seeking or intense physical activity takes its toll on our bodies.

Everybody has a little of this drive. The non-Driven of the world usually have only a modest amount. If a farmer were waiting for the crops to grow and wandered away chasing a shiny object off on the horizon, he'd starve.

If you are Driven, regardless of whether you have one or both alleles, you have always been and always will be Driven. Thousands of years ago, your drive for more and better enticed you to find a better way to hunt, or kept you wandering the world for other environments with better conditions and more plentiful resources. Today, you are still Driven to improve. Where most live by the adage, "If it isn't broken, don't fix it," D2/D4s are of the mindset that, "Broken or not, we can always make it better."

We are wired to master our environment, but because we never feel the full reward of our accomplishments, we have an internal need to seek novelty, risk, and something better. No matter what we do, we need something more. The subconscious elephant may be temporarily satisfied, but eventually gets restless and wants "more." The monkey mind may not be sure what the "more" is, but we will push forward and look for it just the same in the hope that it will finally reward us. We keep coming back, regardless of the challenge. We have a resilience that supports us under the most difficult circumstances. This resilience is the product of another bit of biological magic: Neuropeptide Y.

NEUROPEPTIDE Y: HYPERFOCUS AND RESILIENCE BY ANOTHER NAME

The hyperfocus and resilience characteristic of the Driven and their ability to recover from stressful experiences is associated with a pancreatic polypeptide known as Neuropeptide Y (NPY). This resilience was critical to survival for early humankind. Let's say you are chasing a rabbit and the rabbit gets away. Out of the corner of your eye, you see another rabbit. Wham! The lost rabbit is forgotten, the stress and disappointment is gone, and you are off to hyperfocus on the new opportunity.

If you focused on the rabbit that got away and wallowed in the disappointment, you wouldn't have been ready to chase this next rabbit. You are ready because NPY kicks in and immediately orients your CNS on the present moment, pulling you out of the past so that you can chase that new rabbit.

You can see this reliance in Thomas Edison. He didn't have 10,000 failures. He found out 9,999 ways *not* to make a light bulb. Some might see those trials as failures. He saw them as learning opportunities. He was able to recover from disappointment, adversity, and stress. Most inventors have this ability, as do first responders and others in high-stress careers.

Emergency room doctors go from broken legs to sore throats to car accidents. They thrive in that type of continuous high-pressure environment because they're able to recover so quickly. The time flies by and the stress actually helps them to perform better. This increased performance and quick recovery from stressors can be attributed to NPY.

Neuropeptide Y binds to synapses in the frontal cortex. It

specifically modifies the way the Driven brain responds to noradrenaline. Rather than getting more fuzzy-headed and checked out during stress (dissociation), we become more focused. Our brains literally function *in the present moment* better when we have something to stress about. *New Scientist* (May 2009) did a great recap of these findings, summarizing about the non-Driven:

> Less-resilient individuals, on the other hand, seem to have a lower capacity for NPY production. What is more, their smaller surge of the neurotransmitter during Survival, Evasion, Resistance, and Escape (or SERE is one of the most stressful trainings conceived) training seems to deplete their reserves, causing NPY levels to drop below baseline for at least 24 hours.

Levels of NPY can predict who is going to be successful in strenuous military training. Those with high levels of NPY are 80 percent more likely to make it through Navy SEAL training. In fact, the military are talking about using NPY as one of the criteria used to select the people they send into combat. Those with high levels of NPY will be better able to bounce back from the stress of combat, and may be less likely to develop PTSD.

Hyperfocus and resilience can, however, be a double-edged sword. We can easily avoid the real consequences of our actions. Think about the addict who crashed his car last month. Because he's moved on and forgotten the incident, just as the primitive hunter forgot missing the rabbit and hyperfocused on the new opportunity, he's more likely to repeat the mistake. This quick recovery eliminates what might have been a valuable reminder of the harmful consequences of a certain decision. You may see this in a woman who repeatedly dates the same kind of "loser" again and again. She's hyperfocused on the new opportunity while tuning out the mistakes of the past. Einstein's definition of insanity is doing the same thing over again and expecting different results, but if you have high enough levels of NPY, you will do the same thing over again, not because you expect different results, but because you don't remember the results from those prior times. No wonder high-intensity video games are so absolutely consuming for the Driven. Five minutes into the next mission of Call of Duty, and not only are your issues of the day gone but, along with them, every worry you have.

The majority of people without these gifts do not typically recover as easily from risk and tend to be fairly risk-averse. Again, they can't take the same sort of risks that a Driven can. A farm crop or a herd of goats is not like a rabbit—there won't be another without a lot of effort. If farmers risk trying something new and, as a result, lose their whole crop, it can be catastrophic. Thus, whatever worked last year is what they plan to do again this year. As Driven, we may not only recover from risk, we may actually be drawn to it. Anything that kicks in our NPY is a coping mechanism. The non-Driven look at this as crazy. Why in the world would you want to come home from a stressful day and then relax by doing something stressful? If you're Driven, the stress pulls you into the present and helps you let go. The shooting meditation we discuss in later chapters capitalizes on this Driven gift.

As a Driven, your hyperfocus, resilience, and discontent mean you are equipped to perpetually take a risk in an attempt to make or find something better. You don't tire of trying, and you don't give up. You recover quickly from those failures, those "missed rabbits," or those inventions that haven't yet worked. This is an enormous asset. Understanding how the role of NPY fits into your biology helps in understanding your perception of experiences, and it opens some windows in the ego tunnel.

THE SCIENCE OF SPIDEY SENSE—POLYVAGAL THEORY

Randy was a point man (navigator and pathfinder) for his SEAL platoon. His approach was always to notice personally, as a point man, any issues and immediately react. For this role, he relied very heavily on his gut feelings. He would sense not only with his eyes, ears, and nose, but also with his intuition—a form of extrasensory perception, or spidey sense.

He was often on patrol at dawn or dusk, roughly five meters ahead of the platoon, with no visible or auditory threats, yet, he'd suddenly get the "sense" something was off. Somehow, Randy knew. It was a push away from something, a pull toward something, or "knowledge" from his core.

He'd immediately stop the platoon, and they would kneel and wait. Then he'd get a team of guys to look, see, hear, and feel out their surroundings to validate that gut feeling he'd had. Probably about 95 percent of the time, they would find something—somebody hiding in the bushes, a booby trap, an improvised explosive device (IED), and all sorts of dangers would be there. This saved their lives a few times.

Randy's abilities weren't magic. Many people are able to do this. It's something our bodies have done for thousands of years. Many of us are just out of touch with the skill. Owing to the fact that we are out of touch, that intuition seems rare. But, if we can learn how to build a system around our gut instinct (proactive interoception, or useful interoception, as it's called), we can recapture it. We can begin to hone this skill, along with our other gifts, by understanding it.

The occipital dominance of the Driven gives us amazing powers of observation and skill at noticing the most minor shifts in our environment. We have highly developed systems for quickly determining which way to react. When we catch a glimpse of movement out of the corner of our eye, whether we are aware of it or not, our primitive reptilian brain registers this shift in our environment and responds by increasing our arousal, intensifying our external awareness, and freezing our movements automatically.

Not only do the Driven sense dangers or opportunities in the environment that those without their genetics may miss, Driven people seem to be gifted in the abilities to read and feel in our guts our pack mate's reactions to the environment. Hippies have long talked about feeling good and bad vibes from the people around them. Research is beginning to support that this may actually be true. How this system really works is still much of a mystery, but science is starting to explore and understand what might be happening.

Professor Stephen Porges used his Polyvagal theory as a first attempt to explain the phenomenon of these extra sensory perceptions. Its theoretical complexity quickly goes well beyond the scope of needed understanding to harness our intuitive powers, but a general overview will provide the background you need.

Simply put, the Polyvagal theory describes the role of the two branches of the tenth cranial nerve—the dorsal and the ventral branches. The dorsal branch interacts with the CNS's reactions to danger, and the vagal branch addresses psycho-social heart rate regulation.

The dorsal vagal branch goes from our primitive reptilian brain stem down into our guts. It's related to the fight, flight, and freeze mechanism in the CNS. When we perceive an "oh-crap" moment and everything seems to stop in the body, that's the dorsal vagus nerve doing what it's meant to do. Being able to perceive and sense the slightest shift in movement or lack of movement, triggers our CNS to respond accordingly. Our eyesight is strongly associated with this awareness, so those with visually dominant brains would obviously be better at catching the minute details of an environment.

The dorsal branch is also associated with assessing emotional atmosphere. Think of a large herd of gazelles. If just one gazelle at the front of the herd feels scared and freezes, a wave of fear ripples through the entire herd and they all prepare to scatter. Each gazelle will sense danger and react without actually seeing or even knowing what that potential danger is. They trust their "gut." As an aside, it's interesting to ponder whose feelings you are actually experiencing within your gut when you are surrounded by a bunch of people freaking out. Yours? Theirs? Both? The boundaries among all of us may not be as firm as once believed, especially when it comes to feelings. Feeling the good "vibes" in a crowd lifting your mood is what the 1960s were all about.

Our ability to multi-think enables us to attend to the multitude of minute shifts in facial expression, body language, voice inflection, and the continuous shifts of these variables in groups large and small. We are aware of others' emotions and will make subtle shifts in the presenting style to direct the group as a whole. Some Driven salesmen have the uncanny ability to sell from the platform of a stage; the Driven's occipital dominance, multi-thinking, and gut instincts are in symphony and are at their finest in these circumstances.

The ventral vagal nerve, the other branch of the tenth cranial nerve, connects our face to our heart and sends a stream of information into the brain stem. (We are constantly reading each other's faces for a clue as to what is happening in each other's hearts.) Porges proposed that much of our attachment system can be understood through the ventral branch of the vagus nerve. This attachment is critical to survival, for adults, but especially for children and infants, who are completely dependent on their caregivers for survival.

From a biological standpoint, humans just don't have enough time inside Mom's womb. If we stayed any longer, our skulls could not pass safely through the birth canal. Therefore, we emerge into the world, but we do not fully develop until long after we are born. Because of this, we spend our infancy and childhood as prey.

This means we are dependent on our parents longer than any other animal species on the planet. Until at least the age of nine or ten, if not older, we depend on the herd for everything from food to self-defense. This dependence creates a critical need for attachment; we must feel like we have a trusted herd, or the fear can overcome us.

The awareness of our vulnerability begins even before birth. We sense our mother's level of anxiety and are prepared for the world. It's wild to think about, but our CNS actually begins its wiring as early as six to eight weeks after conception. It makes sense biologically that the mom's uterine environment would get us wired for the world, simply for survival.

When we are first born and hopefully get placed on our mother's chest, her central nervous system starts talking to our central nervous system. Research clearly demonstrates how crucial this is to our long-term health and survival. Babies that are not held, will die; they experience Failure to Thrive syndrome. Not only does our mother help us with the external needs of food and protection, her CNS is actually helping to regulate our CNS. When our social bonding system (the ventral branch of the vagal nerve) finally starts to fully come online, it is laid down on top of this fear-based dorsal vagal system. Thus, we're prepared to be aware of and react to the dangers in our world, drawing on the herd for protection.

As such, a fear of abandonment is one of the most powerful motivators in our social structure. The fear of being left behind is hardwired into us long before our awareness of these feelings even starts to develop. Attachment is critical to our survival. If we feel a secure and trusted attachment, we feel protected. The need to blend in, to feel like a normal, valued herd member, determines much of our behaviors. This may provide some insights as to why, as a Driven person, you are willing to hide your gifts. (As you will learn later in the book, you don't need to hide who you are. You need to find others like yourself and form a herd, a Driven pack, of your own.)

Driven people tend to have a somewhat different relationship to the herd than those without Driven genetics. Although humans all need social attachment, our interactions differ from Driven to non-Driven people, much in the way they differ among species.

Some species, such as gazelles, are largely prey and rely upon fear-driven flight as their primary means of survival. What happens when a cheetah runs into the herd? They scatter and each gazelle is on its own, running in as many directions as possible. While gazelles run from danger, the opposite is true for wolves. What happens when a bear attacks one of the wolves in a wolfpack? They encircle the bear and risk their own lives to save their pack mate.

Why would a pack of wolves choose to fight the bear and risk their own safety? From a survival standpoint, how many gazelles does it take to catch a blade of grass? Just one. But how many wolves does it take to take down an elk? All of them! They must mutually cooperate and hunt as a pack to survive.

As both predator and prey (somewhat unique in the animal kingdom), humans are wired both to run and scatter from each other when in danger, or run toward each other when scared. As a Driven person, you may be more like a wolf in your attachment style than that of a passive herd animal.

You may go far to save those to whom you are attached, despite the personal, physical, or financial consequences. The SEAL Teams and Special Forces guys are probably the best examples of this kind of wildly strong attachment (think about your swim-buddy and how strong the attachment is, and how much you would risk saving him). Humans, though wired to escape our predators, can do incredibly selfless acts of bravery and sacrifice.

It isn't surprising that many of the Driven we (Doug and Randy) have worked with in our practice, recall how many times they have been burned by others and settle into a paradigm of being distrustful of others. Although we have their back and have a fierce loyalty, the others in our lives don't necessarily have our backs. From the Driven perception, at the first sign of a cheetah, the people around us are out of there, leaving us to fend off the threat. Additionally, no matter how often our friends really are there for us, our wiring tells us they always could have done better. We may eventually decide that no person is safe, and no one really has our back. We may feel like we really are alone in this world.

Despite our often-fierce loyalty to our pack mates that may seem like strong attachments, many of the Driven may be using the dorsal system of fear as a primary means of going through the world.

We are afraid of the future. In the present, and only in the present, we are okay. In the present, fear will naturally begin to leave the body. Orienting the brain and body to the present and bringing awareness to the heart stabilizes the gut wiring. This process is actually physical, not psychological. The more you can access your gut and heart wiring, the less fear you will experience and the more clarity you'll have of your life's purpose. The more you practice this focus, the more effective, clear, and purposeful you will become. Later in this book, you will develop your understanding of this powerful practice. You will learn that you don't have to be scared all the time. Understanding your fear is the first step to conquering it.

INTUITION AND HEARTMATH EMOTIONAL ENERGETICS

The HeartMath Institute (a psychology and human performance think tank) proposes even wilder theories about our gut's ability to obtain information. They call it the "heart brain"—though probably it should be called the "gut brain." Clearly, that term is not as appealing and thus not as marketable. According to this theory, the dorsal nerve could be termed the Worm Brain, as it is the oldest and most primitive part of the vagus nerve and of the entire CNS.

There is an old trick for catching a bunch of night crawlers if you're going fishing and you need them. It's called worm grunting. Using a standard wooden stake two-to-three feet long that is pointed at one end and flat on the other, pound the pointed end of the stake about one to two feet into the ground. Then, use a heavy metal file, called a rooping iron, to rub the flat top of the stake, creating as much vibration as possible. Vibrations are sent flowing into the ground through the wood stake. The worms feel this vibration in the ground, become extremely alarmed, and rush toward the surface. As they come out of the ground to get away from the vibrations, you grab them and throw them in the standard old coffee can and go hit the lake.

The HeartMath theory proposes that the dorsal vagal nerve acts like the night crawlers' vibration sensor, picking up vibrations all around us. Similar to the workings of the lateral line on fish or the sensors on a shark's nose, the heart brain is able to sense these vibrations and send them to the brain stem. According to the theory, that vagal tone and heart rate variability are changed by these vibrations. When someone resonates with you, they are on the same vagal wavelength. We are all like tuning forks picking up each other's frequencies and sending out our own.

Learning to recognize your vagal tone and its subtle changes is learning to master your spidey senses. This "vibrational" theory gets most people in the scientific community to collectively roll their eyes, but there is probably something going on that we are not able to scientifically account for yet.

EPIGENETICS, THE INTERNAL EXPERIENCE, AND CHANGE

The human genome, or the two million paired strands of DNA within every cell, is basically a giant software program. It very specifically tells the cell what it's supposed to do. Is it supposed to be a skin cell? Is it a fingernail cell? Is it a hair cell? The genetic coding literally interacts with the cell and impacts how the cell manifests.

A variety of personality traits can also be traced to genetic predispositions. Some people are very extroverted; others are introverted and quiet. Some are logically dominant and others are emotionally dominant. Although people think of genetics as being fixed, epigenetics research provides rich evidence for how adaptable genes are, and provides a new understanding of the interaction between genetics and environment. Very specific gene sequences can be turned on and off to adapt to environmental conditions.

A person born and raised in a very cold climate will have cells that do not generate a lot of perspiration. There is limited need for this individual to cool down as there's a limited likelihood they will overheat in that climate. If this person goes to a very hot climate for a short time, they're going to be miserable, as the hot environment will feel much hotter to them than others who have always lived there. Over time, however, their genes will alter so that they are capable of perspiring more to naturally cool themselves off. The interaction between genes and the environment is an incredibly complex and amazing system.

Genes are indicators of potential. There is a natural selection for those genes that sustain the organism. If you are from a long line of people who lived in hot weather, then it is likely that the genes that support survival in a hot environment are going to be expressed. If, however, you move to a cold environment, you are going to genetically adapt accordingly.

Emotional reactions are also impacted by epigenetic phenomena. Consider a rabbit raised in a valley of hawks for five generations. This rabbit is genetically prepared to live with the threat of hawks. If you move the rabbit to a valley where there are no hawks, this rabbit is going to appear unnaturally nervous, even crazy. It will see hawks everywhere, though there are none. The rabbit is expecting them. Now, if you take a rabbit that has not grown up with hawks and deposit this rabbit in a valley full of them, that rabbit will not survive. It doesn't perceive hawks as dangerous, nor is his level of internal guard appropriate for the environment. With time, the offspring of this rabbit (if it survived long enough to mate) would have made the genetic adaptations to better prepare for survival.

Driven people are like rabbits wired for a world of hawks, but living in a peaceful valley. The rest of this book is a path to hack into our biology and speed up this process of training the inner world to more accurately reflect the outer world.

The brain is probably the most adaptive organ in the body. The key to successful navigation through these changes is the way we meet the world and the way we ultimately understand it. If we approach situations with a preconceived set of expectations, our understanding will be limited. We will be steering our ship with a potentially distorted or inaccurate map of the real world.

We are all prone to the confirmation bias—I expect this, I see it, and seeing it is proof that my expectations were accurate. It prevents us from seeing where our own perceptions are coloring the situation. If, however, our approach is grounded in curiosity and non-judgment, if we actually meet the world with a mindfulness that aligns with that curiosity and non-judgment, we are much more likely to align our internal experience with the external world. This allows us to live in one world—the real world, as opposed to two separate worlds. It lets us be genuine, rather than having a secret internal world.

Learning to take on this challenge, to step outside of our internal experience, requires that we recognize that internal experience and where it derives from. I am neither the elephant nor the monkeys, and I can rewire the elephant and not believe what the monkeys are saying. We must understand that if we don't feel rewarded, it isn't necessarily because we didn't succeed. We must learn to capture those sensations in our bodies so that we can analyze them and determine real danger from a product of our internal experience—perhaps a legitimate issue, perhaps something to see beyond.

· CHAPTER 3 ·

THE DRIVEN IDEAL AND THE DRIVEN REALITY

"Our duty is to encourage everyone in his struggle to live up to his own highest idea, and strive at the same time to make the ideal as near as possible to the Truth."

—SWAMI VIVEKANANDA

The Driven are among the most vulnerable for developing midlife crises. As they begin to get a little more insight into themselves, they may realize that they aren't content with life. Whether they are successful or have problems, they begin to wonder whether they need something more.

You may be one of the Driven with financial security—the house, the wife, the kids, and yet, you still feel like it's not enough. You start to get a suspicious sensation in the elephant that tells you, "You know what? Maybe there's something more here that I'm missing. Maybe it's another woman I need. Maybe it's another business. Maybe it's another hobby."

These Driven can't quite figure out why their outside world looks so great, but their inner world is such a mess and seems lacking. They don't realize that their D2 and D4 genetics leave them feeling unrewarded, regardless of how enviable their circumstances seem. As a result, they scramble to find ways to get their reward so they can feel okay. They hold tightly to the belief that if they finally get out of these field teams or they finally reach the million-dollar mark or the ten-million-dollar mark, or they can finally sell the company, or they meet the ideal woman, they'll be happy.

Most midlife crises develop in the early forties for men and the early thirties for women, but today, people in their mid-to-late twenties experience these same feelings. The introduction of the internet has made millionaires and billionaires of very young people. The Driven have used their multi-thinking skills to launch lucrative ventures; by age twenty-five, they're making a million dollars a year.

By the time they're thirty, they have enough wealth that they have nothing to worry about the rest of their lives. They *are* worried, though. They're suddenly at that point in the horizon where they thought they'd be happy, and they're not. They have no idea what they're going to do next, and it's terrifying.

When you believe the horizon holds your ideal identity, and you reach that point and don't feel right, the dorsal vagal system kicks in generating fear. We can fall apart. As Driven, we are wired to run toward the finish line. We have the tangible proof that we succeeded. The money is ours. All around us, our loved ones are celebrating our achievements, but we don't feel rewarded in the way we thought we would. The outer world might look rosy, but in our inner world, we are still unhappy and scared. We're positive we've made a mistake somewhere, which would explain why we don't feel rewarded. We may even believe we're flawed or broken, and we're ashamed.

The others around us can reinforce this belief. To those without these genetic gifts, we have no reason for our discontent. There's an unspoken (or perhaps spoken) judgment that we should be ashamed for not being grateful for our success. What others don't grasp is that the Driven are dealing with perpetual uneasiness that crossing a finish line won't cure. The disconnect between our inner world and the outer world can bring isolation and loneliness.

Finish lines change frequently for the Driven on their quest to finally change things. The concept of a finish line is probably the single most undermining belief a Driven can embrace. We will examine this in more detail later; but, if you think about it, the Driven who are wired this way will never be satisfied. Better is infinite—we can always be better—but it has no finish line.

Even without the fear-Driven motivation that we must succeed, a Driven's orientation to multi-think (one of our most powerful abilities) can run so wild that it's no longer about finishing; it's about struggling to even start the race. There are countless amazing possibilities all competing for and winning our attention. We are often told we have such potential, but never seem to make progress. Our natural inclinations are to focus on what interests us the most, and to ignore those areas that don't. But those assumptions can result in harmful procrastination. We can spin in all the possibilities, until physical and psychological chaos takes over. Our inner world feelings of dissatisfaction and angst are then substantiated by the happenings of the outer world.

Those without these genetic gifts (think those wired for

safety and sequence) don't typically experience these problems. They are comfortable within their niche in an organization. They labor along at their assigned tasks, and prefer the structure and predictability it provides. They try to impose a framework of predictability into any context. This comfort with structure and the organization seems to be lacking in the Driven.

The Driven, in most cases, find this kind of atmosphere stifling. Structure is reminiscent of their school days with an established curriculum, timetable, and inflexible rules. Yet, as you will learn, the Driven do need structure. The reality is that without a system, the Driven fall victim to the dangers associated with the D2/D4 genetics—the addictions, the broken families, the loss of income. Their midlife or quarter life crises move from storms to full-blown hurricanes, often destroying their lives. The first step in taking charge of your genetics is building the right environment for your personality, giving you the structure you need.

THE RIGHT ENVIRONMENTS

Randy and Doug's friend, Robert (name changed), exemplifies how the right structure can turn a thrill-seeking street thug into a hero. Robert grew up on the streets of Los Angeles and started out as a straight-up L.A. gang member. He was kicked out of high school at an early age, but he was making thousands of dollars every week through his drug sales. But his ability to detect danger helped him avoid the police and mostly stay out of trouble. Once he joined the military and had solid structure—an instruction manual so to speak—he became one of the best operators to date.

Typical of D2s, Robert is impulsive and obsessive. In his Navy SEAL days, you couldn't miss that impulsivity. When the whole SEAL Team played underwater hockey, Robert had quite the advantage. He could hold his breath longer than anybody else. When the team ganged up on him, he'd dive underwater and pull everybody's swimming trunks down, including the commanding officer. When you do that in high school, you are expelled. When you do that within the SEAL Teams, you are just another stellar guy playing to everyone's Driven nature.

Robert is also a great example of a successful Driven that has been able to maintain a gifts-suited environment beyond the military. At the age of forty, he's something of an ideal archetype, has learned about himself and his needs, and has focused these attributes into a rich and fulfilling life. He changes his persona just about every year and has held more jobs than five people combined. He is currently a very successful entrepreneur.

With the right circumstance and environment, the Driven can look like a duck in water, allowing them to succeed. Many of the Driven naturally gravitate toward the military or high-intensity medical fields. The military, in a sense, provides that "instruction manual" for using the genetic gifts that do not apply in most twenty-first century, white-collar environments. In civilian society, the Driven may have incredible trouble fitting in.

The Driven gifts are highly valued in the SEALs. The teams were made for the D2/D4 personality and brain structure, with each day different from the last. The overall mission is as vague as finding, killing, or capturing bad guys around the world. When the time comes for a specific mission, witnessing the hyperfocus of fourteen warrior-Driven minds on one commander's objective is a beautiful event. The intelligence guys are super-focused on the terrain, the enemy, and other factors; the demolition guys are already thinking about what kinds of door charges would be best; the snipers are picking the best rifle for the terrain and distances; and the officers are calculating the contingency plans. It is truly a symphony of warriors focusing their minds and actions on the task ahead.

Once feet hit the ground, however, the realities of conflict have the effect of taking the sheet music of the planned symphony and shredding it. The symphony begins to resemble a jam session and only a Driven's mind can truly reset so quickly. The team guys don't get stuck in what should have happened; they focus only on accomplishing the mission and getting home alive. Almost every real-world mission looks like this.

Of course, there are missed notes; accidents happen and not everyone adapts perfectly. The Driven's mind, though, is the only thing that keeps it all together, the platoon rocking in the right places. Following every mission, open personal accountability sessions (debriefs) work to "sharpen" the team and are just as important as the pre-planning sessions. There is a constant state, in both the individual and pack mentality, of continuously seeking to improve. When this same practice is applied to small entrepreneurial-Driven teams, "crushing it" in business becomes a similar jam session of success.

The heartfelt attachment that the SEAL band of brothers creates together is truly physical in nature. The fierce bond is so obvious among them that it is palpable. The training is designed to build these attachments and reinforce the mutual interdependence amongst the teammates. Looking from the outside, the joking and banter may seem on the edge of cruel; but, underneath, a genuine warmth and mutual respect is clear.

Driven attachments are different from the attachments in a typical cohort. We use the sympathetic branch of our CNS, rather than the gentler ventral branch. A wolfpack in nature demonstrates this bond through play fighting and wrestling. The similar type of bond between these warriors is amazing to behold. You may see a similar bond in the tight knit collective of entrepreneurs launching their startup or firefighters combating a blaze. These environments call for that same split-second thinking, comfort with risk, amazing resilience, and commitment to the team that we see in the SEAL Teams.

THE STRUCTURE OF THE SEALS

Navy SEALs are true D2/D4s, attracted by the present opportunities for excitement or a chance to grab that prize just out on the horizon. Their high levels of NPY provide them the resilience to keep coming back, regardless of the intensity of the challenge, and regardless of the degree of sacrifice.

Most SEALs report that they've always known they were different. They felt a calling toward this warrior's life—a feeling way down deep—and knew this was exactly what they wanted to do. They just didn't know why, or that there is a genetic reason for that calling, for that desire.

Navy SEALs are considered the best-trained warriors in the world. SEALs are idolized more than ever before (though most would say to our detriment). As a SEAL, you are a part of an elite team that is involved in amazing things; you travel around the world having incredible adventures. You're trusted with a tremendous responsibility and feel honored to be able to fulfill it. The rewards in SEAL life are quite considerable, as are the requirements.

Only about 6 percent of those who apply to become Navy Seals are accepted. The requirements, both physical and mental, are unbelievably challenging. You must be in the prime of your life, between the ages of seventeen and twenty-eight, and pass a medical screening. You must meet the scoring requirements of the rigorous Armed Services Vocational Aptitude Battery, which evaluates your cognitive abilities. This instrument tests your knowledge of vocabulary, arithmetic and mathematical reasoning, science, reading comprehension, verbal expression, and your understanding and aptitude in the areas of mechanics, shop, automotive, electronics, and the ability to assemble objects. Applicants' resilience, performance strategies, and personality traits are evaluated using the Computerized-Special Operations Resilience Test, or C-SORT. A SEAL must have high moral character and be able to obtain security clearance. The SEAL Teams are looking through the thousands of applicants they receive each year to find a real-life Superman.

Part of why a young man can become a real-life superhero deals with the organization of the SEAL Teams. A prospective SEAL may have the genetics for acceptance, but it is the training that will transform him from an undeveloped Driven into a master warrior. The structure of the teams include roles for a variety of Driven.

Those with D2 genes, the guys who tend to be impatient and need something exciting right now, are naturally drawn into certain roles, often referred to as "door kickers" or assaulters. They are usually the ones carrying the machine guns. The D4s tend to be a little more reserved, and a little more patient because they're future-oriented. Many of them become snipers. Regardless of their specific function, all SEALs are wired to exist in very challenging environments. Those high levels of NPY allow them to adjust quickly in any situation.

Although many may dream of being an elite warrior, these dreams are likely to stay in the province of fantasy. Most recognize the sacrifices SEALs make, both short- and long-term, in order to become and remain one of these superheroes. They read about the challenges, the impact of family life, of opportunities lost, the financial implications of injuries, the casualties overseas, and decide that this life is not for them. But to a Driven warrior, the teams are a comfortable, beautiful place to be.

Of course, not all D2/D4s become SEALs or go into the military. The entrepreneur is the epitome of the non-military modern-day Driven. They learn at an early age, often from their miserable school experiences, that climbing the traditional "ladder of success" doesn't work for them. They learn only what they want to learn in school; and, in the workforce, they work only the way they want to work. Business feels right to these D2/D4s—whether they are arbitraging products or services, or buying baseball cards in large slots and then selling them at profitable prices. They take risks, often very significant ones. This is the life of a natural entrepreneur. It is in their genetics.

THE NOT-SO-RIGHT ENVIRONMENTS

In the wrong environment, the Driven struggle. Many Driven have had negative experiences in the safe and secure world. Contemporary schools are established with the kind of structure and routine that favor the skills of the non-Driven child.

This is not surprising. Schools educate students for the bigger world. With the advent of the industrial revolution,

the world shifted into larger and larger communities, a
the skills people needed, shifted. Schools of the nineteenth
and early-twentieth century existed to prepare students
for a methodical world. The Driven did not have a place
in these classrooms; their differences were called-out in
this ill-fitting environment. This remains true even today.

Most school activities, then and now, require hours of
methodical, desk-bound tasks alien to the Driven's natural inclinations. The traditional classroom is a world that
demands students pay attention to a single stimulus—to
keep eyes on the board, eyes on the teacher, or eyes on
the paper.

The Driven are multi-thinkers. They are oriented to consider a lot more variables at the same time. Students are
typically reprimanded for multi-thinking. Rare is the
teacher who encourages students to listen to the radio
while they complete their homework. The Driven's
NPY-immersive hyperfocus is at odds with the teacher's
direction to put the activity away after the forty-five-
minute period so a new subject can be introduced. A
certain amount of time is allotted for each subject,
regardless of the student's level of immersion. This can
be exceptionally frustrating for a Driven personality.

The Driven often have a need to see the big picture when

they learn something new. Until we can wrap our heads around what we're trying to learn, we just don't get the point; we don't understand the need for the new skill. So, we may quickly disregard it. If, however, we see the importance of how the new skill or information fits into the big picture, we are able to integrate it into everything we know. The traditional school system presents information in seemingly unrelated small chunks which, for a Driven, may seem like a big waste of time. We learn differently and need to be taught differently.

Many teachers were and still are ill-prepared to work with a child who has a Driven nature. Being constantly hyperaware of the environment is interpreted as "easily distracted." Driven students' need for excellence is understood as obsessive, just as their quest for stimulation is seen as disruptive. The boredom inherent in most traditional classrooms, easily endured by a typical child, cannot be tolerated by a Driven. Taken together, these behaviors encompass the teacher's checklist for a disorder. Coupled with high numbers of children in the classroom and little training, they want nothing more than to "fix the problem."

Labeling children can have harmful ramifications, often carrying a stigma associated with shame. Yet, the practice of teachers pressuring parents to test their children for ADHD happens daily. Such diagnoses can result in Driven students being placed into "special needs" situations. They may additionally be forced to take medication that makes them feel sick, makes them lose weight, and only furthers their feeling of worthlessness and shame.

Behaving naturally, for Driven children, causes embarrassment and punishment. Sometimes, just to feel like they have some control over their lives, these students resort to even more disruptive and extreme behavior. Instead of striving for a better life by taking on challenging goals, they will likely and increasingly shift toward a belief that there is something wrong with them. Making matters worse, the $D2/D4$ genetics may ensure an unrewarded and fear-filled internal experience that confirms this belief, potentially forcing them into feelings of shame and the fear that their differences will be used against them.

Driven kids can learn to adapt amazingly well to the school system. First and foremost, they need to be understood. They need to recognize that they are the way they are supposed to be, and not succumb to the shame associated with feeling and acting different. This can be transformative. Any fear in Driven kids needs to be addressed through insight and practices that make their baby elephants feel safe, and not through medications. The information in this book is for children as much as it is for adults, often working more quickly.

THE FOUNDATION FOR CHANGE AND THE FREEDOM IN STRUCTURE

Although Driven don't like structure (in fact, we may hate it if imposed by others), we do need it until we learn to train the elephant to be less impulsive and scared. The trick is, the structure has to be a perfect fit and a framework that works for us.

On a very macro-level, this hierarchy comes from the military. Even though the SEAL Teams are considered one of the most elite units in existence, they are still part of the US Navy and the military set up. It's a structure the SEALs must adhere to—there's a chain of command. Team guys go to work every day and there are specific expectations. This allows them to excel.

If we are forced out of an ideal Driven environment—we must retire from a career as a pro-athlete or elite military operator—we may struggle to find a new environment that fits our skills. When guys leave the SEAL Teams, they often feel rudderless and lose focus on what they want to do. Rotating out of the military may be difficult for any Driven individual looking at the civilian life of a 9 to 5, W-2 job. They can question who they are; there's a lot of "falling apart." It usually takes these guys a few years to find and build that new framework. It's a rare Team guy who can build a good structure and stick to it on his own.

The need for organization is not limited to those in military environments. If you look at some of the great achievers, no matter how creative or innovative, structure has supported their success. Da Vinci, for example, required periods of study, rest, and play. He had assistants and understudies that kept him on task. We may have extraordinary talent, vision, creativity, but we also need a grounding to draw on these talents. Remember, Driven occipital dominance means we're great at noticing everything—but not so great at organizing everything.

The rest of the world, with frontal lobe dominance, is strong on executive function. They may see things at a micro-level; their focus is on the *what* and *when*. Thus, they are typically not idea people. For instance, the farmer gets up every morning at the same time and does the needed tasks, whether it is tilling the soil or keying numbers into a spreadsheet.

Driven see things in a very big picture, global way. Our multi-thinking hypofrontal brain and D2/D4 genetics have us scanning the landscape for something newer, bigger, better. Without some structure, all the stimuli we're attending to and all the options before us can overwhelm us. Meanwhile, the task we needed to complete remains undone.

If you have no internal organizational system, someone

will eventually create one for you, with deadlines and routines. Chances are, as a Driven, you really won't like it. Clearly, the structure that works for the other 90 percent of the world will not work for us. We need something different.

The key to our success is for us to build an external structure that is creatively loose but demands challenge. If we perceive it as too invasive, we're going to feel trapped. In a very stabilizing and organizing way, we have to incorporate this external structure into our internal world.

We don't want to change that amazing ability to create something new by juggling multiple ideas and connecting the unrelated. We want to focus when we need to. That ability is what the structure provides. Later in this book, you will develop the strategies to create a structure customized just for you.

When our environment isn't a fit for us—when we either have no structure or the imposed structure is wrong for us, the feelings of loneliness and alienation can run wild. We begin to question ourselves, and that's when self-doubt, disappointment, and shame begin to flourish. We feel lost. We feel angst.

The word "angst" means an internal sense of disconnection

from yourself. When we begin to spiral into that place of shame, into that angst, we feel like we are falling apart. We start to hate ourselves—but who do we actually hate? Who is this person? The concept of self is where the problem lies. Just as a gene is not a fixed entity, neither is one's self.

Philosopher Martin Heidegger, one of the most influential thinkers on *being* and *self*, proclaimed when you experience this existential crisis, if you don't kill yourself literally, you have the opportunity to step back and see your different selves over your entire lifetime. There is no fixed self as we typically conceptualize it. What "you" think "you" hate does not even exist as "you" may understand it. As you read ahead in this book, you will realize that you are not that self at all.

THE DRIVEN IDEAL: WHO VERSUS WHAT AND THE LOGICAL CONTAINER

When we reflect on our lives, often during times of great stress, such as a midlife crisis, we ask ourselves, "*Who* Am I?" Such a question urges us to find a fixed external identity. Given our D2/D4 orientation thinking, we're broken and need to be fixed; we can search the planet for some unique identity that will satisfy us. *I'm a teacher, but maybe I should be a lawyer;* or, *I'm a lawyer, but I think I should be an artist.* This questioning can lead us to look for another wife, another home, another job, and we can repeat this process in an endless cycle of disappointment. The issue is not with the answer, but rather with the question.

When we ask *who*, we are focusing on the self as a fixed entity apart from the world. This isn't the case. We're not separate—we're part of the earth. When you look at a pack of wolves, do you ask *who* they are? No, you ask *what* they are. They are wolves and they are animals, part of the ecosystem.

Einstein's got a great quote that perfectly expresses this. He reminds us, "Look deep into nature, and then you will understand everything better." We are not separate entities apart from the earth. We are connected to the earth. Einstein also tells us, "We cannot solve our problems with the same thinking we used when we created them." When we ask, "*Who* am I?" we are using the same thinking that created the problems. The question we should ask is, "*What* am I?" This is the foundational question for the logical container we need to build to stop the questioning self.

You are wired as a primitive hunter. You are Driven. As D2/ D4s, we are wired to feel discontent. We hyperfocus and get over things in a flash, as we focus on the next thing. We may be driven by various states of fear or anger. As you have read, this drive is a survival mechanism. Being alert for danger means a better chance of surviving that pre-agrarian landscape and not ending up as prey to powerful and dangerous animals. If we believe that safety is a visible point on the horizon and we run toward it, we are setting ourselves up for failure and despair. When we finally reach the place we can't wait to get to, in order to feel safe and relaxed, it will have evaporated.

We find ourselves still scared. We've struggled toward ten different goals, we've reached half of them, but none have made us feel safe. What we hoped would bring relaxation and respite did not. We've run an unending race. The horizon only exists because the earth is round, and what D2/D4s are actually doing is just running around the earth. They've lost their compass.

Safety is not a fixed coordinate on a map, just as *who* we are is not a fixed identity on a lifeline. That type of thinking, that type of question, has created the problem. The truth is, you're okay now—you're the way you're supposed to be.

Believing that we are not connected to the world (which is illogical) is where the problem originates. Solving the problem with the same questioning, "*Who* am I?" will fix nothing. This kind of illogical circular thinking tells us that once we finally reach the shiny thing or the identity on the horizon—we finally get the PhD, get through BUDs, retire, make the million, or sell the company—then we'll have the answer and be content.

The problem occurs over and over. These guys, these Driven, build up a great company and make tons of money, but then they get bored. They change direction in their company, possibly tear the whole thing down just so they can rebuild it again. They get stuck in a loop of self-destruction and self-creation because they're constantly on a treadmill looking for that happy place, and thinking, "That wasn't it. It must be this. That wasn't it. It must be that."

The Driven who ask, "*What* am I?" get a different answer with a different perspective. They answer, "I am Driven." They understand that this unsettled feeling is normal. They say, "I am different. I am wired to feel like I'm never enough or it's never enough, and I'm always looking for something better. If I keep running towards some magic place over the next hill believing that this is the location of safety and happiness, I'm going to wind up back in that same spot."

When we ask this new question, this *what* question, we are forced to take an inner journey of developing an authentic and true self. By seeing outside of our internal experience, the Driven can ask, "What is driving me? Is it fear? Is it anger? Do I really have a belief system that the castle on the horizon is my nirvana?"

Driven D2/D4s who are able to step out of their internal experience to ask *what* rather than *who* are on the path to recognizing that nirvana is right now. They begin to believe, "You know what, there's really nothing wrong right now, *and* I am wired for a path of constant improvement. I am okay now, but I will continue to make life better."

They are finding *Dasein*, a German word, which means to be fully present in your whole existence. It is through this state, this focus on the present moment that we can begin to feel and ultimately know that we really are okay. It is a challenge, but then, as D2/D4s, we are always up for that.

· CHAPTER 4 ·

REAL LIFE STORIES

"Success is not final, failure is not fatal: it is the courage to continue that counts."

—WINSTON CHURCHILL

When the Driven thrive, their gifts bring extraordinary outcomes for themselves and society. The trick is to harness those gifts to work for us, rather than undermine our efforts. Knowing what you now know of the Driven and the incredible determination they possess, you may have identified many well-known genetically-gifted people who have used these gifts toward great achievements.

ELON MUSK

Elon Musk is an archetype for being Driven. He started

his financial business as a co-founder of PayPal where he made the bulk of his money. From there, he moved on to co-found SolarCity, next Tesla, and then SpaceX.

Musk is smart, highly gifted, and Driven. His dissatisfaction with the current paradigms led him to design and develop revolutionary ways to complete transactions, to obtain energy, to drive, and to go into space. He could have easily retired from PayPal as a very wealthy man without ever having to work again. As a Driven, this wasn't a choice he would or could make.

People like Musk have both of the genetic D2 and D4 markers. They want excitement right now, and they want to change things to make the future better. This means rejecting the status quo. PayPal upset the financial industry. Tesla, a startup car-manufacturing business, is upsetting the auto industry, and SpaceX is again upsetting the aerospace industry with an offering to make space travel affordable for everyone. Like other Driven people, Musk shakes things up.

A multi-thinker who clearly craves the excitement of a new idea, Musk has a vision of the future, which he continuously moves toward. His D4 is also apparent in his wandering lifestyle. Born in South Africa, he has lived in many different countries, including Canada and the U.S.

Musk has a proven history of interdisciplinary amalgamation, meaning he takes ideas and concepts from all over the place and connects them into a new idea (just like the authors of this book have done with biology, psychology, sociology, cultural anthropology, evolutionary psychology, philosophy, and spirituality). Musk understands physics. He understands business. When looking at problems, he understands the problem within the context of a domain, but brings a solution outside of that domain.

The "hyperloop concept" is an ideal example of the result of interdisciplinary amalgamation. We've all seen the drive-through banking window where you put those little envelopes in that air chute. Your envelope shoots through the tube and goes to the teller. This concept is the idea behind hyperloop. Hyperloop is in the domain of public transportation, but draws on the engineering domain that's used in banking to figure out how to transport people over long distances extremely quickly, cheaply, and powerfully. Musk looks through a business lens, thinking about how this works in business, and does the same for physics and civil engineering. He thinks about how to build his idea throughout a region or state, or even a city. One must have the multi-thinking skills of a Driven to be able to do something like that. Most people wonder where all these crazy ideas come from. To most of the world, someone like Musk looks like a superhero.

Interestingly, Elon Musk is the inspiration for the super-hero Tony Stark in the Iron Man comic and movie. Once people hear this, they typically recognize the connection and shared traits. Elon is somewhat of a genius. Pair his intellectual gifts with his hyperdrive and you're getting into the realm of Iron Man.

However, even superheroes have problems. Musk's are well-known: He's been divorced twice. He's had personal struggles. The gift that has catapulted him to celebrity status, that has empowered him to change the world has also put a strain on his life. Clearly, however, he has the structure to harness these gifts; and, despite the challenges and negative consequences, he has achieved success beyond most people's dreams.

STEVE JOBS

Steve Jobs, co-founder, chairman, and CEO of Apple, and a CEO and majority shareholder of Pixar, is another good story—a D2/D4 hyper-driven entrepreneur whose contributions have changed the face not only of technology, but society as well. A dissatisfaction with the existing computer operating system—the kind of dissatisfaction inherent in the Driven—inspired Jobs and Steve Wozniak to build the Mac. In a series of advertisements, a counter-culture mindset is conveyed showcasing the Mac as a young, hip, smart, confident guy in jeans and a T-shirt, while the PC is as an older stodgier man in a suit, bewildered at his vulnerability to viruses, clearly an emblem for the past.

Jobs built Apple and then grew it. He had a perfectionist reputation and was well-known for being something of a jerk when it came to getting things done. If something wasn't perfect, he'd throw it in the trash. His Driven instincts kept directing him to make it better with an almost obsessive-compulsive fervor.

Everything Jobs did had to be the best. He had his fingers in the design, the creation, the marketing, and the sale of every piece of gear that came from Apple. It is rare for a CEO to be so hands-on. His products were new and innovative, and every piece was well designed, from iPods to iPhones. After he was fired from Apple, he started Pixar, where he brought his same drive to the movies. Pixar was sold to Disney for $7.4 billion. Jobs was then called back to run Apple.

Jobs's obsessive-compulsive perfectionism is not uncommon in D2/D4s. These types often develop OCD tendencies, which helps these individuals control their multi-thinking; it gives them a focus that functions as a constraint for their tangents. The OCD becomes a way of harnessing and self-governing this thinking which, if left unchecked, could become counterproductive or destructive. It helps manage the fear underlying the drive for living in a scarier world.

Having a structure, even one like OCD, can keep a Driven on a productive track. Steve Jobs in his early years was deeply involved in practices to focus the mind. He was skilled in meditation and used this tool as a philosophical guide. He carried this discipline into this work, seeing his business as something aesthetic. At an early age, he was able to control his mind to be able to focus on how things really are, how they look inside, as well as outside. This philosophy or construct became a tool he used to harness his gifts.

Cultural dogmas often view the world as it should be or the way it used to be. Presenting styles of meditation attempt to look at the world as it really is. This is a powerful approach as it diminishes the difference between an internal and external reality—between the fantasy of what should be and the reality of what is.

WOMEN AS DRIVEN

Driven genetics are not specific to gender. Laura (name changed), Olympic snowboarder, reflects on her experience as a highly Driven woman.

Laura knew at the age of twelve that she was more Driven than most. Securing the track and field locker key at school to practice her high jumps during odd hours, she wanted to become "the best." Laura was not so Driven by the result of the competition, as by the feeling of intense competition. She parlayed that highly Driven impulse into a variety of sports—track, competitive horse riding, and then snowboarding.

Laura comes from a family of D2/D4s. Her father, a racecar driver, was highly Driven. But like many D2/D4s, he hadn't learned to harness his gifts and suffered from addictions (alcoholism and gambling). Though her father earned a top income much of his life, he had very little to show for it.

Initially, Laura's need to be rewarded also resulted in some negative behaviors, and she was kicked out of three high schools. She was, however, able to recognize those tendencies and establish some critical boundaries, building her own set of practices to handle her powerful drive. At an early age, she recognized that her own "container" needed to be tight, and she would have to guard against the negative manifestations of her genetic gift. These disciplines were the key.

Laura learned the paradoxical truth that discipline equals freedom. She knew her powerful energies must be channeled correctly and addressed constantly. She had opportunities to learn these techniques through her travels and multicultural experiences—spending time at the Shaolin Temple in China, practicing Kung Fu and meditation, making nine trips to India, studying yoga, and finding herself in the hospital multiple times following her snowboarding injuries. She and her young child go on short adventures to places like South America.

An epitome of a Driven, Laura's qualities are front and center, displaying both the DRD2 and the DRD4 genetic allele traits. Her history of being "paralyzed by perfection" is an indicator of some of the OCD traits manifesting at the higher ends of the Driven spectrum.

As is common with D2/D4s, multi-thinking is just a part of who Laura is. She is a master at talking, sensing, and thinking at the same time. She may be simultaneously talking with another executive about a programmatic detail while thinking of the strategic posturing of the move, the tactical practices needed to execute it, the personality types and specific people needed to perform it, and the fact that she needs to summarize this information in writing for the executive. While the connections of multiple conversations and concepts in any one moment might drive most people crazy, she sees the connections and their importance to the present moment.

Most people would be almost disabled by such a powerful gift, but Laura's introspectiveness and ability to constantly ask "why" have allowed her to productively channel her gift. She was ranked first in Australia and tenth in the world as a snowboarder. Her companies are thriving, and she continues to kick ass as she continuously learns who she is, how her gift affects her, and how to build on her strengths. Although we've seen many successful D2/D4s, Laura stands out as someone extraordinary in channeling the gift though powerful introspection, curiosity, and self-discipline.

Laura is now the executive of a very successful chain of yoga studios and married to another Driven. Their young child may indeed have those same genetic traits, but only time and experience will tell.

Driven women and men face the same challenges associated with D2/D4; however, being a woman does have additional implications as the consequences of the drive are different. It has been our experience that Driven women's social struggle is greater, primarily due to the stigma associated with being a female powerhouse. Hyperactivity in males is more accepted: The "boys will be boys" attitude prevails in most cultures, generally excusing their impulsive behavior. Additionally, men are more heavily encouraged to play sports; most sports support the Driven's need for excitement and their focus on the future, the next game to win.

Social expectations for women are more aligned with the conventional world. Although this is changing, the traditional role for women as homemakers, secretaries, nurses, and teachers are a fit for those content with the status quo, and do not crave thrills or seek adventure. Women true to their Driven instincts are more harshly judged by the world.

Friendships can also be more difficult for Driven women. Laura struggled to get along with other women. Most didn't trust her. She was always Driven to be the best, and she was impatient and dissatisfied with what the world considered acceptable. These qualities were often interpreted as bitchiness. She realized that she got along a lot better with men; all her best friends were men. Even other highly Driven women became adversaries; though, occasionally, they connected and developed a friendship.

Sometimes the easiest way to cope is to hide those gifts, but this tactic always leads to shame and disappointment. Thankfully, Laura didn't hide her drive—she learned to adapt it, channel it for the given the situation, and apply it appropriately. She's been able to make life as a highly Driven female work. Being a female Driven can be a great advantage. While societal expectations can be toxic, occasionally they work in their favor. Think of the different ways men and women approach learning physical skills, such as shooting. Men often bring their ego to the lesson, believing they should be able to master the skill quickly. This mindset becomes an obstacle to learning. When they pull the trigger, missing the shot indicates to others and themselves that they're a failure or a fool. They are unable to fully focus on the target because they worry about how the experience will impact their ego.

Women, while sometimes fearful, do not typically have ego issues related to these physical skills. Unlike men, they are not worried about feeling incompetent if they miss a shot. Their multi-think skill is highly sensory and introspective—how their right brain, left brain, and body all integrate to be able to shoot. They're focused on the present—the sensation and integration of the mind and body, typically outshooting men in target practice.

During a shooting meditation course (we will discuss in later chapters how this is *the* way for a Driven brain to learn to channel their hyperfocus while relaxing at the same time), Laura excelled. During one of the last cycles of shooting meditation, she had a bit of a competition with one of the men. He was not just any man. He was a long-time Navy SEAL veteran with hundreds of thousands of rounds fired in practice, if not millions (we pro-bono SEALs in our courses).

This was Laura's first time shooting a gun. It was the end of the day, and she had fired at least twenty-five rounds, increasing from 50 yards, to 200 yards, to 400 yards, etc. until the finale at 1,000 yards. She fired her five rounds right before the SEAL. The significant left-to-right cross wind from five to eight knots, with gusts to twelve knots, would push the bullet two-and-a-half to almost six feet to the right, which is not an easy shot on a thirty-square-inch steel target.

With her previous experience reading the wind, Laura followed procedures for relaxing the body, used her years of meditation and focus practices, and brought it all together to hit the first three shots. Her dopamine was soaring and a smile of deep satisfaction was on her face. Her adrenaline got the best of her on the fourth shot, and she missed by three inches on the right. She later reported that the chattering monkeys thought she could go "five-for-five," which kept her from being present and self-sabotaged her shot. A wave of frustration and self-judgment went through her body. She harnessed her drive and focus and quickly used her NPY gifts to let the past fall away. Her intensity was palatable but she was completely relaxed. With ease and grace, she corrected for wind and focused;

she let out her breath half way and let the fifth shot go; dead center, and four out of five.

With glee and full-embodied satisfaction, she got up from the gun and returned the thirty feet back to the meditation cushion where the other shooters were in Driven meditation. As she was getting up from the gun, Randy touched the former Navy SEAL's shoulder, signaling him it was his turn to shoot. He got up and slowly did a walking meditation to the gun. As Laura walked past the Navy SEAL, the aura of energy around her couldn't be missed. Just as they passed, they made eye contact, her glowing face and a giant smile was magnetic. She instantly raised four fingers to him, which she immediately followed by a fist pump. The SEAL's face half-grinned, knowing immediately she got four-for-five, and then his smile shifted. The Driven are very competitive.

As he witnessed Laura's success, the SEAL's face took on an intensity that only a twenty-year veteran with multiple deployments can muster. He approached the gun with complete conviction and promptly pulled his first shot to the right and missed. He came off the gun with amazement and frustration, and committed to slow down and not miss again. The next two shots hit near center mass and the steel could be heard ringing back. The fourth shot was a hit also, but at the far-right edge—on target by just one inch. The fifth shot was one of the most memorable battles of ego we have ever witnessed.

The SEAL's investment in the future and his drive to be a success were at odds with what we had been teaching all day, that, "Every shot is just one shot." We repeated countless times that if you trust the body and the brain to follow the procedure, the results will be better than you can hope for. He lay behind the gun for minutes (we shoot in prone position), which seemed like an eternity. The tension in his body was climbing. You could almost smell the glycogen burning in his brain. He took four or five deep breaths and, collecting the multi-thinking mess he had become, got back on target. He eventually pulled the trigger, intensely focused on just accelerating the trigger to the rear in a smooth motion. His hyperfocus on just this one aspect of the experience caused the change in wind to go unnoticed. He missed, hitting only three-for-five.

He began to laugh at "himself" as he recognized the *real* problem. It was ego. It was not the first time his ego had sabotaged him, but this was the first time he had witnessed the battle within so clearly. During the debrief, he stated with a laugh that he had "one f-ing monkey that just would not shut up."

Women seem to have a clear advantage in their ability

to listen and trust that their efforts will lead to success. They recognize we must be in the present, focused not on future wins or losses, but the actual act we are performing. Beating a Navy SEAL during her first time at shooting added to Laura's satisfaction. She trusted that following the process and staying out of the results leads to success.

DRIVEN AMONG US

Not all D2/D4s are celebrities. Ted (name changed), a first-generation Mexican-American, began to live parallel lives early in his life. Growing up in the "hood," he quickly recognized that *smart* and *tough* did not go together, and the key to survival was to keep his intellect a secret. His neighborhood placed no value on education, so Ted adapted accordingly, developing an aggressive persona at home with his alcoholic and abusive father and on the streets with his friends.

When he was kicked out of public school in the second grade, Ted's parents enrolled him in a private Catholic school. Here was a place where education was valued, but of course, outside of the classroom, he was mocked by his "homies" as a "private school kid." He drew on his adaptability, secretly excelling in school while maintaining his ruffian lifestyle in his personal life.

Ted always had entrepreneurial leanings. He got his first

business opportunity when he was in third grade. In order to afford the private school, his mother worked at the rectory and he was an altar boy. One day, he stumbled upon a cellar full of wine that the priest had on hand. Realizing there were too many cases for the priest to keep track of, he began selling some to his "homies."

In high school, the students had to wear a tie every Friday to go to church. Students who didn't wear a tie served detention or were paddled. Ever aware of entrepreneurial opportunities, Ted bought a box of ties and, each Friday, rented them out for a dollar each. This went on for years. Making money was always easy for him. He recognized what others needed and how he could capitalize on that need.

That he was different never occurred to Ted; he simply thought of himself as a poor person with a survival instinct. His ability to adapt was strong. He lived as a stellar student, athlete, altar boy, entrepreneur, and ruffian hanging out in the "hood." He even played the part of Fagin in his high school's performance of Oliver (a role that cost him his cool card, but sparked a love for theater that was to continue).

Ted's habit of always saying yes to any opportunity, alongside a bit of bluffing and boasting, won him a two-year contract with the Comedy Club in Los Angeles. He promptly dropped out of college to pursue the entertainment industry, television commercials, and he ultimately started a production company. Ironically, this stroke of good fortune was also his first brush with the dark side of his drive. Ted enjoyed success at comedy and at running a production company; he had lots of money but, by the age of twenty-two, he was a college dropout living a life of drugs and alcohol. He had the incredible gifts of the Driven—the creativity, the ability to multi-think, and the appetite for something new, but he had no container. They controlled him, rather than the other way around.

Fast-forward through a return to college, some freelance writing in New York and a return to San Diego, his next pursuit was running a real estate firm. Again, the dark side of his drive surfaced.

When he was focused on his business, nothing else mattered. He'd wake up, smoke two packs of cigarettes a day, drink coffee, slide into a martini, and finish the day at 3:00 a.m. The next day would be more of the same. "I ate a lot, drank a lot, messed around a lot, and took on projects no one else wanted." At one point, both the Mexican and Chaldean mafia wanted to talk to him. He loved it, though. To him, this was living. However, his lifestyle was taking a toll on everyone around him. His marriage fell apart and his daughter was hurt in all the dysfunction.

He couldn't sleep. He couldn't function. He had flashbacks of things he couldn't actually remember. He was afraid he was losing his mind. He was an adult, a CEO of a company, but the onslaught of his childhood began to attack. He became a scared little boy. Ted calls it, "An incredible breakdown." He sought help, found the process, and began building the needed logical container.

So began Ted's journey back to health. The process helped him slow down and catch his impulses. He quickly grasped the simple elephant and monkeys model. He stopped the personal narrative of self-attack and his outrage at others. Through meditation, he discovered how to control his gifts. At first, sitting quietly for two minutes was the most difficult and horrible thing he had ever done. His initial discomfort became an intense need. He began with two minutes, then five, then ten, and then the impulsive urge to escape from his inner world began to subside—his inner and outer world discrepancy started to resolve.

Ted ultimately realized he was different from those around him. Initially attributing this difference to his eagerness to say yes to everything that came along, inside, he suspected there was something more going on.

He's come to learn that he loves crisis and chaos; it's where he functions best. Ted realizes that he has always been

Driven—he was a soldier without a war, and had PTSD from a childhood of trauma he'd locked away.

In the past, he never slowed down enough to take pride in what he'd done. He never stopped to be grateful and live in the unearned peace beyond our understanding—grace. For the Driven, it can be extremely relieving to know we don't have to prove ourselves in order to be free from stress. This is a different and ideal way for a Driven to approach the world.

Like Ted, Jack (not his real name) is also Driven. He realized he was different, highly Driven, in his early teens. He began immersing himself deeply into sports. First, it was Taekwondo. He became the youngest black belt in the country. Next, it was snowboarding, professional cycling, and running. He called it, "Chasing the rabbit."

Jack loved long races far above team or stick and ball sports., favoring cycling and cross-country, anything requiring "a lot of suffering." He was always his own competition, trying to beat his personal record.

Although he hated school, like many D2/D4s, he got decent grades. He planned to go to law school and even took his LSAT but, right before submitting the online application, he literally pulled the power cable on the computer. The thought of being trapped in the routine of law school for another three years after his undergrad was nauseating. But he felt lost, unsure about what else to do. When all his fellow seniors were interviewing for jobs in corporate America, he felt absolutely no desire to go down that path. Instead, using his final college semester's tuition money, he started his first tech integration business. Juggling web design, SEO, and marketing for companies, he also attended courses.

Throughout Jack's life, his drive for more—more education, more money, to be better—conflicted with pressures from his friends and family to follow the "normal" path for young men his age. He seemed out of step with the people in his life. He saw only mind-numbing boredom in that future. This conflict quieted when he would run, but only during the fifteenth or sixteenth mile. He had to push himself so hard to get relief from his inner world that he suffered physical injuries. These days, his "dopamine fix" comes from skydiving every weekend. This is when his monkey mind is clearest. He is removed from emails, cell phones, and agendas. His only responsibility is pulling his chute, and that makes life simple.

Jack's been meditating about six months. It started as an easy addition to the morning routine: Get a cup of coffee and sit down on a cushion. Meditation has moved him into focus and enabled him to drop into a flow state where the inner and outer world fall away, without having to go to extremes; although, he still likes the extremes, too. Driven meditation has manifested in a lot of self-discovery, clarity, and inter-connectivity for Jack. He likens it to using the GPS on his phone—when he first looks for a location, he sees only the street he needs. Meditation helps him hit the "zoom out" button until he sees all the roads that connect—all the pieces to any problem at hand.

His path in the future? He plans to continue as an entrepreneur moving from the digital space to the product space. Meditation will remain a part of his life as he continues on the path of personal discovery, enjoying each day as it comes.

These stories aren't about people getting over addiction. Rather, they're about highly Driven people who recognize that addictions, problems, and negative consequences are just the result of a powerful drive running uncontrolled. If you're a Driven in middle school or high school, and you're stuck learning from a traditional model—locked in a world of conventional mentality—you are going to struggle and may find yourself doing things that get you in trouble.

The predisposition to need something better or to look

toward the future is ultimately grounded in the primal dissatisfaction that manifests as *drive*. We have the potential for great stories, like those of Elon Musk or Steve Jobs, but we need a structure that aligns with the Driven urges, yet keeps us on track. When that framework is absent, it can lead to bad stories.

Clients who haven't found structure and can't direct their drive fall victim to addictions from gambling to drugs to sex. These addictions promise relief from the endless, almost obsessive-compulsive desire to be better—to get to the anticipated point on the horizon. The drugs, sex, or alcohol offer respite from self-perception as failures, beliefs confirmed by falling short of societal and self-imposed expectations and not grasping that coveted prize. Their disappointment is crushing proof of their inadequacies.

Highly Driven people need the right environment, and the right design for their "high-powered" drive. Envision a Formula One race car. If you put this super-charged machine on a downtown street, you're going to get into trouble. Take that same race car and put it on the Indianapolis Speedway, and it's a perfect fit. Understanding your drive is the key to overcoming and avoiding addiction. You want to put your gifts in the right environment, an environment in which a Driven individual can thrive.

· CHAPTER 5 ·

YOUR OWN WORST ENEMY: SHAME

"Now, many people who don't know a lot about trauma think that trauma has something to do with something that happened to you a long time ago. In fact, the past is the past and the only thing that matters is what happens right now. And what is trauma is the residue that a past event leaves in your own sensory experiences in your body and it's not that event out there that becomes intolerable but the physical sensations with which you live that become intolerable and you will do anything to make them go away."

—BESSEL VAN DER KOLK

When most people walk into a psychologist's office, they have a problem to solve. They may not know exactly what the problem is, but they do know the struggle is an inner world kind of hurt that needs to be fixed. Often, they use drugs, alcohol, work, thrill-seeking distractions, women, men, whatever they can come up with—but nothing works. The feeling just intensifies. And while they try to deal with it, eventually it builds to a level beyond what they can tolerate. They can't solve the problem on their own. They are living a bad story, believing a bad personal narrative. At this point, hopefully, they make that appointment with the psychologist.

Occasionally, these people come into the office to tell the doctor, "I want to kill myself." At these words, most therapists tend to drop their jaw in apprehension and concern. Doug's initial reaction is, "Great, I will show you how." The goal of such a response is to distance the person from their concept of the self. At the very least, this unexpected reaction encourages them to become curious about what it means to kill oneself, to question what it means to hate oneself—to ask who is this *self.* Doug's comment isn't meant to minimize their pain and suffering. The purpose is to shock them out of their belief that the *self* and the body are one and the same, creating the opportunity to step out of the personal narrative.

For some, it's the first time they've awakened to this new possibility—the concept of the monkeys or the elephant. In their attempt to answer, they become the curious observer who is neither monkey nor elephant.

Ultimately, this understanding is the first step toward recognizing that—despite their current feelings—nothing is actually wrong, nothing is broken. Their constant worry about future consequences, and their intolerable internal sensations (the monkeys and elephant combatting within), can be set aside. In that moment, sitting in a nicely appointed office in San Diego, the logical fact is that in this moment, they're safe. While this pill can be nearly impossible to swallow, as these clients ponder the *I am neither monkey nor elephant* answer, the sensations in the body begin to calm the elephant. Breathing becomes softer, shoulders begin to settle, and even the chattering monkeys take a break from the attack.

This shift toward the safe outer world (which is presently an unarguable and logical fact) and the dissolving of the inner world can be profound—even tearful for those who have spent a lifetime trapped in the inner world. However, most of the Driven who come into this office aren't tolerant of the safe present for long. The elephant quickly becomes restless.

As you have learned, their internal experience—the D2/

D4 reward deficiency and chronic discontent—raises the belief that something is wrong. They think, "Something doesn't feel right; therefore, there must be something wrong with me." Then, any bad things that happen on top of this will fuel the fire, or support their belief that there really *is* something wrong. Trauma, or the perception of trauma, accelerates this self-hate. In a sense, the bad event is the proof that the self truly is defective; otherwise, such bad, traumatic things wouldn't have happened. As you have learned in prior chapters, the unwanted event confirms for us our defects and our flaws, and with this confirmation comes a horrible, dark shame.

TO HELL AND BACK: DARK SHAME MONSTERS AND PSYCHOSOMATIC DISORDERS

Jeff, a teen with powerful D2/D4 gifts, experienced this shame when trauma struck. Like so many D2/D4 genetic hunters, he lived with a strong drive for more, for better. He was a thrill-seeking adrenaline junkie with enormous reserves of NPY. Yet, he struggled with the feelings of boredom and unease, believing he'd find contentment if he could just complete the next major challenge. As a freshman in high school, he believed the social conditioning from his parents and teachers—that if he performed well in school, he would get into the best college possible, which would then lead to a successful, happy life. The belief in this truism seemed very real and important to Jeff. He is Driven.

Jeff's goal was to work the system rather than have the system work him. He understood that getting into an Ivy League school was a brand for life and, despite the stupidity of the system, that could help his success in business.

Determined to give himself every advantage, he set up an appointment with a psychiatrist where he was tested for learning disabilities, knowing that having a learning disability would entitle him to a variety of financial support. He told the doctor he had trouble concentrating and took a long time to finish the tests, which was true to a certain degree. Five hours later, he was diagnosed with ADD and Slow Processing Speed. Now, he could take a pill, and was entitled to extra time on the standardized tests. He had a competitive advantage over his peers. His moral compass had shifted. To Jeff, this didn't matter. As far as he was concerned, the new advantage was more important—he had to look the best to get into an Ivy.

Despite the accommodations, he still scored in the thirtieth percentile of the ACT score, something which embarrassed him and, until now, he didn't speak about. After taking the ACT six times, he eventually learned the test and reached the ninety-ninth percentile. He was a varsity basketball player with perfect grades and test scores—the makings of a killer college application—but that wasn't enough for him. He had to go further.

He started an environmental club to show his leadership capabilities. This involved filling out a three-page form and inviting his friends to do a beach cleanup. He also hired experts to help him write his college essay. He had grades, test scores, evidence of leadership ability, a strong essay, and athletics—all he needed for a bulletproof college app. He was accepted. Then an accident changed his life forever.

Jeff had always thrived on the excitement, energy, and freedom that high-risk situations brought. For as long as he could remember, he was hooked on this feeling of thrill-seeking. As young as seven years old, he would beg his parents to drive him to the mountains so he could learn to snowboard and attempt the forty-foot jumps he'd seen in movies. Within a year, he was winning snowboarding contests and received a sponsorship.

When his family moved from the mountains of Colorado to the beaches of San Diego, he took up surfing. Dropping in on big waves, a giant wall of water trailing behind him ready to crash at any moment, gave him that moment of peace, too. As a senior in high school, he would surf at the famous Blacks Beach in La Jolla. However, there came a point where surfing just wasn't giving him the same rush as it used to. He had to find the next thing to conquer: The sky.

He hiked up the four-hundred-foot cliffs from Blacks Beach to Torrey Pines Gliderport, leaving his surfboard behind. He started paragliding lessons. Within three days of ground training, he was allowed to launch. It was absolutely exhilarating. An uneasiness that lived within him craved the "in-the-moment" feeling of jumping off cliffs. He had finally achieved the dream of human flight. He felt free and invincible, as if there were no boundaries. However, like with any D2/D4, things escalated quickly.

He inevitably pushed things too far. There's an old saying with extreme sports that if you look for your edge, sooner or later, you will find it. It's sort of like a drug user who needs more and more to achieve the same high, and eventually, there's the crash and burn.

People didn't understand his attraction to the sport. Friends of his parents disparaged this inexplicable risk-taking. They had no understanding that for Jeff, a D2/D4, extreme sports were a drug, an escape from the drudgery, boredom, and accompanying uneasiness that comes with day-to-day living.

The weekend before his flight to Yale, his paragliding instructor offered an advanced paragliding clinic in Utah. Jeff immediately signed up. His parents had always been lenient and were usually supportive of the decisions he made. They agreed to let him paraglide as long as he never rode a motorcycle. However, just to make sure they didn't veto his plans, he told them he had signed up for a "Safety Training Workshop," instead of the "Advanced Acrobatic Clinic." His little stretching of the truth worked. Three days later, he and his family were on their way with camping gear and paragliding equipment stuffed in the trunk of the car. Jeff eagerly joined the class, innocent of what awaited him as he took to the skies.

The last thing he heard before falling into a death spiral was the paragliding instructor on the radio telling him to brake. Jeff had no time to pull the reserve parachute. The instructors had him doing wingovers only three hundred feet up. It would have been safer if he had been at three thousand feet.

It was a long way to fall. Jeff spiraled out of control and hit the water at full force. The wind was knocked out of him. He found himself underwater, terrified, strapped into his harness, and tangled in thirty tiny strings from the paraglider. It took a few moments of lying still for him to comprehend what had just happened. He suddenly realized that he didn't have much time to spare and had to figure out how to get untangled. The buckles came off surprisingly easy, as did the lines. He swam up for air.

Still dizzy, he scanned his body for injuries but couldn't find anything wrong. He wasn't even in much pain. At the edge of the lake, a couple hundred yards away, his parents, the paragliding instructors, and other students were waving, hoping he was okay. The paragliding school boat, which was supposed to be close by, was on the other side of the lake already towing the next student up thousands of feet. Joseph, one of the instructors, attempted to rescue him, but after swimming twenty yards realized there was no chance of making it in time and swam back. Five minutes later, the owner of the paragliding school showed up on the boat teasing Jeff, attempting to lighten the mood.

Back on shore, Jeff noticed a pain radiate down his spine, but he wasn't alarmed by it. When the other students asked him how he felt, he brushed aside their concerns, though still shaking from the incident.

Later that day, he decided to fly again—something that he reflects on as being completely outlandish. His parents were shocked and so were the other students in the course. The paragliding instructors, who were also D2/

D4, encouraged him to get back out there. He believed himself invincible, not knowing that his crash had fractured his back in four places, the heightened adrenaline covering the pain.

Once he hit three thousand feet, he released the tow rope and was on his own again. The instructor had him do a full stall. He grabbed the brakes and started slowing the glider down. At the instructor's request, he jammed them to the bottom. The wing crumpled into a ball and he started free falling. The paraglider re-inflated and jerked him back to a stop. He felt pain radiate through his spine. He knew he shouldn't be doing this. He flew down. The ordeal was over.

His back remained sore throughout the week. In fact, it got worse. This was the start of years of struggling with chronic pain—commonplace in America, but most common in the D2/D4. Not only because of his risky thrill-seeking behavior, but also because the mind seeks to protect itself from the toxic emotions that come with shame. The physical pain is the answer to the D2/D4's perpetual quest to find something wrong.

"I wouldn't wish this pain on my worst enemy," he said during his first visit with Doug. Chronic pain is real. The agony, limitations, fear, and frustrations of the constant burning, aching, and jabbing pain can cause people to lose all hope. *Not Jeff. Jeff never felt like a victim, but he became consumed with finding an answer.* This was the next phase of his relentless drive to fix something that he thought was broken—his body.

He was committed to curing his back pain. He met with world-renowned orthopedic surgeons, physical medicine and rehabilitation doctors, pain management doctors, chiropractors, acupuncturists, physical therapists, and osteopathic physicians. When their pain meds, injections, MRIs, exercises, and manipulation weren't working, he set out on an alternative path.

He had preconceived notions that any healthcare provider whose name didn't end in MD was a scam artist; however, in the face of pain, he would try anything—crystal healing, body work and massage, hyperbaric oxygen chambers, plant medicine, movement classes, electromagnetic stimulation, hypnosis, and reiki. To his frustration, his pain continued.

Despite the physical agony he endured daily, he still had his eye on the future; he still had his obsession to go to an Ivy League college. The Ivy remained the perfection he sought—the shiny trinket on the horizon. He believed Yale would set things right in his life. He would have to manage the pain, while continuing to look for answers. He fixated on his studies, earning a near 4.0 GPA, despite his constant pain and his struggle to stay focused in class. He often hid out in his room with no social interaction, enveloped in self-hatred, pain, and fear. He believed he was broken on many levels, and thus that he was unlovable. He was certain he was stuck here. Truly living in hell on earth.

Jeff finished Yale in only three years, driven by the graduation he saw as the shiny prize. If he finished Yale, if he got all his work done, then maybe he'd feel okay. This drive was grounded in shame, the shame of not being enough. It's a shame that drives genetic hunters into the shadows. The shame that, if unchecked, spins somebody off into helplessness and hopelessness, relieved temporarily by drugs, alcohol, or, in Jeff's case, a toxic perfectionism. It was a specious promise of internal contentment because of his perfect external world.

D2/D4s have a fantastic ability to take ownership of problems. In the library, during the last week of school at Yale, he was seen by classmates reading *Gray's Anatomy*, the old, iconic, seven-hundred-page anatomy book. They were perplexed by his choice to read such a book, especially considering he was a finance major. But, he eventually found the cure to his pain and, to his surprise, it was not through anatomy, but through psychology.

Not able to sleep that night, he turned to his laptop, skimming through back pain blogs, and he stumbled upon a controversial doctor out of NYU who seemed to have a cult following. His name was Dr. Sarno. After looking through thousands of five-star book reviews from people with similar stories, he clicked "Buy Now" on Amazon.

Dr. Sarno, who is now retired and in his nineties, spent his entire career as a physical medicine and rehabilitation doctor. However, just like many of his patients, he, too, was frustrated with the lack of effectiveness of the methods he learned in medical school. He also noticed that many back-pain patients had similar personalities. They were all extremely motivated perfectionists, and the majority of them had prestigious careers and educations. Like the authors of this book, he too believed that a lot of successful people were motivated by social pressures and feelings of insufficiency. Furthermore, he believed that to the subconscious mind, emotional pain (such as shame) is tremendously more terrifying and toxic than the tangible feeling of physical pain.

A fan of Freud, he believed the subconscious mind is quite powerful and runs much of our life, going to great lengths to avoid feeling shame. The mind would go so far as to create physical pain to distract from uncomfortable emotions about the self. He coined the phenomenon as

Tension Myositis Syndrome (TMS), often describing it as an evolutionary glitch, a psychosomatic condition, or a self-protective mechanism. "The pain is real. It's not that it's in your head," he would explain, it's that "the root cause is the subconscious mind." It was there for a specific purpose—to distract. Unfortunately, it was doing more harm than good.

As Jeff read through the pages of Sarno's book, *Healing Back Pain*, he saw himself in the descriptions. What if the same D2/D4 genetics that caused the original paragliding accident also caused his mind-body disorder? The escapism from his boredom to begin jumping off cliffs, the escapism from being just Jeff to becoming an Ivy League scholar, and the escapism from his emotional pain to causing the distraction through physical pain all followed suite. Over the course of the next month, he learned how to address the psychosomatic phenomenon described in the book, and his pain finally subsided.

He realized that he would have to start the process of going into his shame, rather than running from it. Perhaps exposing it to sunlight would cleanse him. Keeping shame in the darkness would only cause it to proliferate, like mold in the basement. This would require more bravery than jumping off cliffs, and more discipline than his academic pursuits.

We asked Jeff, at age twenty-five, to give us a brief write-up about where he is today. It follows:

I was at the meditation retreat with Doug and Randy deep in the sequoias. There was a stark contrast between the sweet forests with birds chirping, and my inner world in its chaos.

Sitting still with an empty mind was no easy task. In fact, I was facing dragons of shame and discomfort. But by the end of it, I had one of those "Ah-ha" moments.

Every time my thoughts started to drift, I became more and more frustrated. What the hell? How do I only have the attention span of a three-month-old Labrador? I can't even stay focused for more than thirty seconds.

I was like a pressure cooker that was on the verge of exploding. Then all of a sudden:

"Who cares?!" I thought to myself. Who cares if I'm not as good as the bald eighty-five-year-old Japanese monk sitting across from me deep in meditation? No one was watching me as closely as I thought they were.

"Who cares?" I said to myself over and over again. Who was this "who," anyway? Then a list of things I was

ashamed about started through my stream of conscious-
ness. I couldn't help but laugh hysterically at these things.
I was literally laughing at myself. The self and I became
free of each other!!!

Who cares that I was still living off my parents' nickel?

Who cares that I hadn't dated anyone in the last
six months?

Who cares if I'm starting to go bald?

Who cares if I can't put on weight/muscle when I go to
the gym daily?

Who cares if I spent my whole life trying to escape the
present moment?

Who cares if my ex-girlfriend...

Who cares if...

I laughed and laughed. My sternum area that held so
much tension freed up. I became lighter. I thought I was
floating. Tears rolled down my eyes because I simply no
longer cared about my own opinion of myself.

I remember something one of the old-time surfer mentors "Rodrigo" once told me: Never forget your ABCs.

"Always Be Cool."

Being ashamed of myself constantly is not cool; seeking validation in the outside world is not cool; and the amount of pressure I put on myself daily my whole life was not cool. And that rubbed off on others socially. I had always wanted to be that cool, popular guy, but had too much shame and was too attached to outcomes. I finally felt that freedom I had so desperately sought.

This wasn't the end of all shame in my life going forward, but I knew for certain that shame was something that I could live without. Every time I experienced shame, I said NO.

Shame is a toxic thing that shouldn't be allowed to exist on planet Earth. I would imagine myself launching the shame into the sky through galaxies far, far away to this stinky ugly planet called Planet Shame. This is the only place in the universe where shame is allowed to live.

I invite everyone to launch their shame to this planet.

I found my work to be more productive. I had fewer

attachments to ideas, less swirling around in fear, and less concerned about life outcomes, and more fascinated by the process of living and achieving. And there was freedom knowing that my success didn't define me. I noticed how much easier it is to have fun and be grateful, which was worth it regardless of whatever I achieved. It was unconditional. This sense of fun and gratitude became my secret sauce to alchemy.

I directed my ambition like a sniper, the same way Doug and Randy had taught me during their meditation shooting courses as I started at one of the leading consulting companies. I had directed focus, while keeping my lens wide and open to not miss opportunities for work and play. I was tired of suffering, and I just made a commitment to be done with it. I played in the cornucopia of the world, and took the brave step of just being grateful for all that I had and all that was on its way.

Having the awareness that I was a D2/D4 and wired differently than most people who I engaged with on a daily basis helped tremendously throughout this process. It gave me freedom to accept what I am, to engage in the world on my terms, ultimately owning what I am. My D2/D4 was a source of my power when harnessed intelligently. Here are a few examples of profound changes that I noticed:

- *When my friends sat around watching a movie on a random Friday night, I would usually complain about it and try to convince them to come out, have fun, and get outside of their comfort zones. However, this time I just accepted my differences as a D2/D4. I just left them behind, went out to a bar, put myself in an outgoing and powerful state, and created the experience and life that I wanted (despite how socially challenged I was and how awkward going to a bar alone made me feel).*

- *I posted on social media without the guilt, fear, and feeling like I'd be judged. I realized that everyone wasn't watching me, and I thought my ideas and posts would benefit others.*

- *I noticed I had less grandiose desires, and I was less delusional. My desire to build and own a business, rather than sticking with management consulting, was less about achieving unlimited money and power and creating a façade for my insecurity. It was more about creating a lifestyle that worked for me while doing something impactful. It was that simple.*

It's true that despite all the changes, I still feel that every second of every day has to be productive. And it's true that having mile-high goals adds a lot of pressure. This is not an easy life of a D2/D4.

However, as a D2/D4, I deeply accept what I am, an engineer of my life in a way that this intensity is focused and empowering. No more jumping off of cliffs, no more cheating the education system, just honest and relentless hard work to make things happen that I want, and scheduling time to work out, surf, socialize, and care for myself. And of course, not taking things too seriously, so I can be that cool confident cat I always wanted to be.

Trauma and D2/D4 genetics seem to parallel each other. As genetic hunters, we are designed to live in a world that is much scarier, much harder to survive in, and much more traumatic. While we cannot definitively say whether trauma or perception of trauma triggers these genetics from an epigenetic perspective, we do know the interaction between nature and nurture supports this connection. As Driven, we are prepared for trauma; it is possible that traumatic situations ignite or amplify the impact of having these alleles, with outcomes that may be better or worse. Better because our higher levels of NPY support the resilience we'll need to cope. Worse because we're more sensitive to danger, aware of risk—and better able to juggle those tens of variables that factor into a traumatic situation.

The D2/D4 drive that can catapult us to success can also function to drive us into the ground, when not appropriately harnessed. Jeff had some strategies to cope with the boredom of everyday life. He needed the risk he was born to expect and thrive under. Extreme sports initially worked for him as a way to introduce a hunter experience into his ill-fitting farmer life. The risk was his drug, his way of numbing himself to the shame and discomfort of feeling broken. When he started to apply his drive in the right direction, physical recovery and optimum health became his obsession. He is a great example of the old saying, "When you're in a hole and build a ladder to get out, the top of the hole is just the beginning; the ladder continues up into the sky."

· CHAPTER 6 ·

STOP SABOTAGING YOURSELF

*"The ability to observe without evaluating
is the highest form of intelligence."*
—JIDDU KRISHNAMUTI

Research on lottery winners reveals that most people who win $5, $10, and $20 million wind up in debt or bankrupt. Their stories are incredible and well worth Googling. Most winners go on subconscious and impulsive spending sprees, making horrible investing decisions, and often being swindled out of their money. They buy houses that are too big and they can't afford to maintain; they buy more cars than they can afford; they create a lifestyle that isn't sustainable. This applies to 90 percent of all lottery winners.

Why do they do this? Why do we sabotage ourselves? Why is it so hard to change?

As discussed in earlier chapters, we have an inner world, one that includes the personal narrative running in our heads, the collective opinions we hold about ourselves, and our feelings. The belief that this inner world is the *real me* or is *reality,* and the subsequent disconnect between this inner world and the outer world is what produces and maintains self-sabotage.

The lottery winners' experience demonstrates just how powerful these disconnections can be. They never experienced earning this money; therefore, in their internal world, they're not wealthy. They never felt the reward connecting their behaviors to earning this money. Their internal world is incongruent with the external reality of wealth. They sabotage themselves until the money is gone so that the external world maps to their internal one.

Their families end up being disgusted with them, thinking they've squandered this great opportunity. Family members judge their recklessness believing they themselves would have made smarter decisions. Everyone believes that if given such a chance they would use the money wisely. "That wouldn't be me! I would do it differently!" Yet, if these families had the winnings, chances are they too would sabotage themselves (though knowing that you might, changes the odds in your favor that you would not). What most of us don't realize is that the sabotage is on a subconscious level. Our elephant biology just can't handle so much change.

D2/D4-Driven people's core sense that something is wrong or missing is what feels normal. The elephant holds onto this comfortable and familiar state of tension, fear, and anger.

The disagreement between the monkeys and elephant applies to every area of our lives. You may do very well with something, such as a doctoral defense, but your gut—the elephant—tells you something different. The elephant is used to things feeling wrong. Thus, you'll hear the reminder in your head that you were successful only because nobody saw your real, flawed self.

We want our inner world and the outer world to align, so we will subconsciously and sometimes consciously bend the outer world to confirm our inner world. A successful doctoral defense can only mean that we must have tricked those on the committee, because we know, at a gut level, there had to be something wrong.

We *know* that our flaws and inadequacies must be the *real* truth. As a result, we act to align that outer world with our inner world. As long as we're stuck in that loop, we're going to continue to sabotage ourselves. What we need to recognize is that we are not that personal narrative; we are not those opinions or feelings. We are not the elephant, the monkeys, or the observer. We are all of them and none of them.

THE PSYCHOLOGY OF SELF-SABOTAGE

Our mother's internal world, as well as our father's and mother's genetics, lays down the initial wiring for our subconscious self. Her elephant (including her fears and anxieties) wires our elephant while we are in her womb. We are born prepared for the world she inhabits. This makes sense from an evolutionary perspective.

Over the hundreds of thousands of years of our evolution, we primarily used our feet for transportation. Even if we migrated a few hundred miles, it took weeks for there to be a slight change in our environment. Over our lifespan, our environment and social groups changed very little (particularly when compared to today with the opportunities to travel to completely different worlds). We needed to be biologically wired for the area we were born in and the social group we relied on for survival.

Recall that a rabbit born in an environment of hawks is likely to be scared of hawks even before it has seen any—this fear is in their wiring. It's no different with humans. Those of us with Driven genetics are looking for hawks. If there are no hawks, we create them.

The Driven are prepared for danger, but they aren't prepared for the life that is safe, predictable, and calm. Rather than risk letting down our guard, we establish circumstances that require us to maintain our guard. We do these things to confirm our inner sense of what the world is like, which in the Driven universe is dangerous, or at least busy and stressful.

We take on more work than needed; we over-commit to people we don't like; we run late to everything; we find our gas tanks running on empty with no opportunity to fill them. We keep the same relative levels of debt, no matter how much money we make. The subconscious elephant sends up impulses, and the physical resistance needed by the monkey mind creates this familiar world—a world of proverbial hawks. (It is this need for busy, more, and better that creates the superheroes, and the wealthy individuals that some of us become.)

The hardest thing for not only the Driven, but all humans to learn is that our subconscious-self—our shadow, the elephant—is really the one in charge. But the Driven have to burn this truth into our consciousness, or else, we sabotage like no other.

Being able to catch that subconscious-self is key. We need to develop the capacity to feel the resistance to the positive and the impulse to chase dopamine, no matter the consequence. This logical container is the first step toward change and toward empowerment. Without it, we continue to self-sabotage—we continue to create danger and maintain drama. It's what feels normal to us.

BANDWIDTH

Recall that our minds are not our brains; our minds are in every cell, in our entire body, in our CNS. As you have learned, our subconscious elephant (really our CNS below the nose) functions like invisible radar looking for patterns that match previous experiences. When a pattern is matched, the elephant gets a "radar ping," generating sensations.

Within nanoseconds, these sensations and impulses go up to the monkeys, to that newer brain, where they're interpreted as emotion. The monkeys then connect these emotions to a cause either inside or outside of the body. This can get confusing, because the elephant doesn't know the difference between the fear associated with a near-accident on the freeway and the thrill of a roller coaster. There is just the sensation of fear. Making sense of the sensation is the job of the monkey mind.

The elephant has a theoretical, subconscious center point at which it experiences the world as "normal." The space above and below this center point constitutes a bandwidth. The elephant likes to live in the middle of the bandwidth, where things feel familiar. This is also where the monkeys believe they are in control.

We subconsciously resist behaviors that push us toward the top of our bandwidth—behaviors that create safety and success. Likewise, we resist behaviors that push us toward the lower end of our bandwidth—behaviors that create trouble or failure for us. When things start to get to the edge of the band in either direction, the elephant subconsciously begins to dysregulate, increasing resistance to things that will push us outside of what feels normal. Just as we automatically resist touching a stove, we also subconsciously resist saving money if the elephant feels this creates too much safety.

As our world becomes too positive, safe, or successful, we have a harder time doing the things required to maintain this positive, safe world because the elephant is too far from the center—too far from comfortable. If the monkey mind believes this increasing resistance to be valid or reasonable, and thus rationalizes it, the subconscious elephant gets its way and creates behaviors that push us back. We subconsciously resist saving money by believing the monkey mind's rationalization that we need to impulse-buy right now.

When circumstance takes you in either direction, whether winning the lottery or experiencing a trauma, you will have increasing impulses to move toward the middle of the bandwidth—either by doing something positive and productive, or doing something to sabotage yourself, both consciously and subconsciously. As you move back and forth, you tell yourself a story as to why it's okay to be living between these two ends. We have all told ourselves, "This is just *who* I am."

This movement between the bands occurs back and forth, moment to moment, day to day, year to year on both the micro- and macro-levels. There's always this dynamic tension in the elephant keeping us in the familiar zone. We get our desk organized, we clean our house, and then, uh-oh—we're too close to the top of the bandwidth, so our car becomes a mess. We go to the gym faithfully and eat well for the first couple of weeks, but that starts to move us too far to the top of the bandwidth. We eventually quit going, and return to eating bags of chips in front of the TV. This moves us toward the lower end of the bandwidth, until we suddenly see that we've gained twenty pounds and recognize we need to do something about it.

When things are not going well, in reality, we should feel anxious and motivated for change. When the elephant is scared for genuine and controllable reasons, we can focus the monkeys and make a change to reduce the fear. If you're driving too fast on a slippery highway, you want to slow down; if you're starting to dip into your savings, you want to be more careful with your money.

When things are really going well in your life, that's when things get interesting. As our CNS ramps up, and as we get closer to the top of the bandwidth, it's less likely we're able to make an accurate assessment of reality. This is the real problem with completely believing what the elephant is telling us. The elephant may feel a ping from a perceived snake, when it's really a rope; or worse, we perceive things as ropes, when they're really snakes.

Getting to know your CNS is extremely important. When CNS arousal starts up, even the reason is not obvious. At times, monkeys stuck in a state of boredom can come up with very creative rationalizations to explain the fear. All animals struggle with helplessness. Humans, with our massive problem-solving brains, are probably the worst. Rather than sit with free-floating anxiety and experience helplessness to stop it, we eventually find or create a reason for it. We will turn ropes into snakes all over the place.

When the CNS becomes heavily dysregulated and begins moving toward the top edge of the "normal" zone, the monkeys and elephant start to wrestle for control. Thinking speeds up. The body buzz starts to become apparent, and we might have difficulty making decisions. Our speech may get jumbled and our memory may get spotty. As the elephant starts to take over, we start using our outdoor voice. Our posture changes and we get all puffed up. We may get snarky or snap at others easily, or even become tearful at hallmark commercials. Our fuse gets shorter and shorter, meaning we are closer and closer to having the elephant take over all our behaviors.

Anyone who has had a panic attack or a bout of out-of-control laughter can testify that when the elephant gets too ramped up, the monkeys on his shoulders are going for a ride. When the elephant's world starts to become too safe or too scary, as we get pushed or pulled out of our bandwidth with more stress, eventually the elephant will completely take charge.

If stress continues, or the monkeys believe they are totally helpless to stop the stress, the dorsal system kicks in and the elephant goes numb. We may seem to be functioning, but the elephant is no longer getting radar pings as it should. To protect itself, the elephant has disconnected from the real outer world (dissociative). Then, when we are safe enough to feel again, the CNS dysregulates, attempting to reset its bandwidth to the center point. This is essentially what occurs in Post-Traumatic Stress Syndrome (PTSD). This can be alarming to the monkey mind if the elephant has been numb to these sensations for some time.

Combat veterans with multiple deployments need to grasp this as logical reality so they can recover. When they ask, "Why am I freaking out?" Doug and Randy answer, "Your world is now safe enough in *reality* to allow it." The numbness is gone. (This also explains their impulse to go on another deployment; for them, the experience of combat feels normal.) It may also force them to bounce from one hyperfocused situation to the next situation, where the NPY keeps them feeling somewhat normal. When they don't have this intensity, the elephant is uncomfortable.

The CNS, a miracle for survival, wants us to heal. It wants to get us back to "normal." But without this *logical* understanding that the inner world isn't an accurate reflection of external reality, we create reasons for the freak-out moments that make sense now. We want to go back to where the elephant feels "right."

Those of us who are Driven feel normal when things *don't* feel right. If things start to feel right, we subconsciously push toward the more comfortable center point on our bandwidth which, for us, is a place where things are dangerous or risky, where we need to draw on our Driven gifts. There are countless stories of entrepreneurs and pro athletes building up amazing lives in short periods of time, only to have them come crashing down.

Many therapies and "life change" programs love to rile up the monkeys and train them to override the impulses and the resistances of the elephant. This approach works temporarily. Neuro-Linguistic Programming, for example, works for a while, but you need to sign up for the next course to keep the monkey mind driving the elephant in the right direction. This makes an amazingly successful business model, one that has helped many. But the elephant eventually wins. You have to get down below your nose to the source of the resistance and not make any story, positive or negative, about the elephant's messages.

Increasing your bandwidth is gold. Everyone wants to avoid "losing it," to be sure the elephant doesn't take charge. A narrow bandwidth means you will be closer to the edge of losing it all the time. The closer to the edge you are, the more likely your CNS is getting dysregulated—the elephant's impulses and resistances will be greater, and the monkeys will more likely try to change the external world to match the inner world chaos. But before you can worry about working on the edges of the bands, you need to find your center. The stability of your CNS is key to life change. When the elephant is calm, your thinking is clear and problems are easily solved. For most of the Driven, this is rarely the case. The next chapter is dedicated to stabilization. We'll get there soon.

THE LOGICAL CONTAINER

The logical container holds your experience in a way that can be seen and understood from a distance. It allows you to stand as an outside observer and laugh at your own humanness. With a basic understanding of your biology, hopefully, you can hear the monkeys chatter, feel their different moods, and observe the elephant's sensations and impulses. Perhaps most importantly, you can meet them with a logical curiosity, one that asks what's happening without making a judgment. With time, you will begin to see the sabotage in nearly everything you do. You'll observe the elephant and monkeys telling you that you're not in the mood to go to the gym, or check your email, or clean the kitchen, or finish that paper. You'll experience the sensations in the body. These sensations will almost instantly travel up to the monkey mind. You may start to hear a rational argument, a logical reason why it's okay to grab a beer and watch the game instead of heading to the gym; to leave the dirty dishes in the sink; or to let the research paper go another day, because the DVDs your kids put in the wrong boxes, as usual, really need to be organized. It's amazing how much procrastination can accomplish when there's an important task we're resisting.

Learning how to break this cycle requires us to catch this process before it turns into behavior. In doing so, you're not only empowering yourself to change, you're rewiring both your hardware and software system and literally changing *you*. Once we know the biology of emotion—beginning with the sensations and impulses of the elephant, then the connection of these sensations and impulses to mood states, and finally to the rational story we use to explain those emotions—allows us to interrupt the cycle at any point. Although this happens in a flash, with practice, we cultivate a Mastery Mindset of curiosity and constant improvement, which allows us to control this cycle. The mystery of our subconscious elephant and monkeys unfolds right before our consciousness. If you want to be in awe of what this skill looks like after years on the Master's Path, read Josh Waitzkin's, *The Art of Learning.*

This path starts by simply observing our typical patterns. My elephant gets a ping to the radar, which results in an impulse to be on guard. The elephant will respond by bracing my shoulders, and I will feel a slight tightening in the diaphragm, making my breath slightly shallower. This response goes up to my right hemisphere, my emotional self. If I confirm it—if I believe in it, and believe what my body and my gut (dorsal vagal system) are telling me—that what I'm doing is actually really scary and dangerous, my right hemisphere will then confirm it. If there is in fact something dangerous in the present moment, then my system is working, and everything is fine.

If, however, my Driven instincts have me believing in a dangerous landscape when, in reality, there is no danger, then my inner world will break from the outer world in a negative way. In this situation, I'm no longer using clues from the outer world to determine the truth of what's happening. Instead, I'm choosing to believe the biases from my inner world. If I quickly scan the environment, my emotional bias will selectively note information that confirms these emotions, supporting their reliability and their truthfulness. I will literally see only those things that validate the inner truth. This is a big problem.

There are many examples of this. A guy in Northern India knows there are King Cobras all over the place, and he knows they are dangerous. He gets out of bed and puts his foot down, landing on something that feels long and tubular-shaped. Immediately, his limbic system uses pattern recognition and identifies a match to a King Cobra. His reflexes kick in and he recoils his foot and jumps up onto his bed.

The elephant has done its job and *his world is safe again*. But the man's body feels this incredible amount of tension and fear, which comes up into his neocortex, to the right hemisphere. If he chooses to believe in this information, he panics and runs out of the room. If he chooses instead to become curious about it, he will be able to look down and confirm whether or not his inner world is accurate about the outer world; he may see the harmless tie to his robe. He won't disconnect the inner and outer world—he won't tell himself, "I feel anxious, so therefore, there absolutely must be a danger here." He'll be able to stay within the bandwidth, able to tolerate the situations, and he will stay in reality.

We are fear-based animals. We know that a hot stove is dangerous. We recognize this danger from prior experience, from prior trauma recorded in our body and brains (along with the reaction we need to keep us safe). As D2/D4s, we are wired to live in a world of proverbial hot stoves. Every time you walk into the kitchen, you have an ingrained resistance to touching the stove, even if it isn't on. This is a wonderful attribute that has kept our species going for thousands of years; but it also has liabilities, in that we're afraid when there is no need to be. What will free us from this possibly constant state of fear and being on guard is a logical container to hold this experience, this fear, and then we can meet the real world with curiosity. That curiosity will allow us to check whether the stove is on or off.

As D2/D4s, this logical container of curiosity is critical. We are, by nature, at risk for trying to subconsciously self-sabotage—our inner world working to align our flawed self-perception that says, "Something is wrong" using evidence from the outside world. It doesn't have to be this way. If we can feel the subconscious self (elephant), feel the emotional self (monkeys), and then catch those feelings before we act and be curious about it, we give the logical self an opportunity to do a reality check. It empowers us to compare the inner world and the outer world, and to assess the accuracy of our inner world.

BUILDING INTEROCEPTION

When they first explored the relationship between meditation and shooting, Randy and Doug (both with years of long-range shooting experience) discovered something very special. Shooting meditation provides the best way to experience the differentiation between the three selves and the moment when all three selves *fall away* into one collective whole sense of self—a selfless self. The inner world and outer world split and *fall away* into one whole world, with you completely in it.

The experience is similar to surfing, skiing, skydiving, fighting, rock climbing, or any activity that forces you into the present. However, unlike these activities, which require present focus for survival, shooting meditation is a conscious step-by-step process in the quiet safety of stillness. Shooting meditation allows for internal neurological mapping to occur, which enables the student to access this flow state in any activity they choose. The ability to get into this flow state is the ultimate tool for the Driven person. We are naturally inclined to be hyperfocused and to multi-think, but our fears, easily-bored CNS, and compulsive need for dopamine get in the way of most meditative techniques. Yet, the shooting meditation technique is ideal for us. It aligns with our ability to hyperfocus, it addresses our need for dopamine, and it is challenging enough to hold our interest.

Why is the process so unique? Let's explore how the different minds (selves) within you react. When you prepare to shoot, your elephant (subconscious self) is naturally afraid of the upcoming recoil, of getting smacked in the shoulder by a big rifle. Your monkey mind is also going to engage; the monkeys will vary their reactions depending on how well or how poorly you're doing. If, for example, you hit the target two times at 1,000 yards, and you've got Navy SEALs or your buddy watching, an overwhelming need to hit it the third time is generated. The emotional self becomes much more invested in the outcome. This experience provides an opportunity to change that investment from being fear-based by directing focus into the present moment, noting how your body feels as it gets ready for the shot, and recognizing what you need to be doing in this moment and only this moment.

In order to consciously integrate all of the splits in our consciousness, you start with the *logical self* and let it simply observe, just be present, without fighting amongst other parts of consciousness. This helps you understand that what you're doing isn't dangerous, and what you're doing for the third shot is no different than what you did for the last two. If you trust the process and perform your third shot exactly the same way as the previous two, and account for changes in the wind, you'll be able to calm the body and hit the target.

We aren't the ones who invented this system of integrating the *selves*. The Japanese have practiced this skill for hundreds of years. One of the arts they've used to this end is *Kyudo*, the art of archery. Granted, we've dissected the biology and psychology behind the process, dramatically speeding up the learning curve. We have also adapted it to our modern culture using precision weapons at long distances. We've come to learn that the crucible of controlling a minor explosion (60,000 psi just inches from your face) with your body creates a much more acute insight experience that is easily applied to all areas of your life.

The process is very much an integration of shooting with a highly specific style of presenting meditation. Literally, Randy and Doug's clients go from the meditation cushions, to a walking meditation, to the gun, through the shooting process, and then return to the cushion. As with *Kyudo*, entering the gun, mounting the gun, shouldering the gun, and finally shooting the gun is done in a sequence of meditative steps. From the time you sit on the meditation cushions, which are thirty feet from the guns, until you return to the cushions, it is one meditative process.

Throughout this meditative shooting experience, Doug and Randy often notice clients manifesting various forms of self-sabotage. They may jerk the trigger, or tense their bodies unnaturally. Some shooters even close their eyes and pull the trigger. Maybe they are hoping for some type of magic to happen. This same self-sabotage shows up in their normal lives, usually on a daily basis.

The internal neurological mapping the client can experience behind the gun is extremely unique and applicable to life, particularly for the Driven and our NPY. In trusting the process, taking a unique style of breath, and hyperfocusing on the moment, the center point of the bandwidth is no longer an issue. There is no longer a split between the monkeys, the elephant, the steel target at 1,000 yards, the gun, or the body. The experience of time expands and the trigger can seem to pull itself. Clients often describe the experience of intuitively *knowing* the target is hit before the gun goes off. This end to self-sabotage is mapped in the body and brain and can be applied to every area of life. Applying it to every area of your life and being in a constant state of learning is the Masters Path. The person riddled with fear and suffering from the imposter syndrome may have great resistance when starting this Mastery Path. However, the logical container frees us from this fear and resistance.

MASTERY FOR BEGINNERS

We don't have to follow a path of self-sabotage. By recognizing where the self-sabotage comes from and understanding its internal evolution, we gain control over our impulses and begin to have choices over our behaviors. When we're watching TV and we suddenly get that uneasy feeling and have the impulse to do something, whether it's cleaning the house, looking at our email, or going for a ride, we have to be able to take pause. We have to stop long enough to assess what is making us uneasy or afraid. As Driven D2/D4s, we have to ask, "Is that just my D2/D4 talking?" This isn't to say that stoves aren't hot or that there aren't real snakes in this world. You just want to be able to catch that fear impulse so you can evaluate it. You want to be able to ask, "Is that stove even on?" "Is it really a snake?" Sometimes it will be.

Impulsive spending is most certainly a snake. You tell yourself that you can't pass up this incredible deal, that you can't afford to not spend the money, that you need to buy whatever it is on sale. If you keep this up, if you buy everything that looks like a great deal, you're going to run yourself into debt, end up living in clutter, and you'll definitely mistake the snake for the rope.

You need the ability to catch yourself morphing the snake into a rope, and vice versa. You need that curiosity. Curiosity is a judgment-free question zone; we just want to ask; we just want to know. We don't attach a value to it. Being able to ask with genuine curiosity allows our logical self to work with more information. This is the initial step in Mastery.

Next is a shift towards the Mastery Mindset. The Mastery Mindset means giving up *who* you are and accepting *what* you are. It's learning how to drop out of the personal narrative in your head and to drop into your body. *What* you are, is *what* you are doing in this exact moment. You are a person reading this book; you are a person stopping to enjoy a beautiful garden; you are a teacher; you are a father; and, if you are a Driven, you are someone who's not going to be satisfied with just one rose in that garden. This is what you are in this moment, and this moment only. When we look at things through the lens of *what* rather than *who*, we lose the self-judgment of *me* in the future and in the past. This is a very powerful, key concept of Mastery.

You are focused on this moment, whatever this moment is. You're taking a shot at the steel target 1,000 yards away. You're not thinking that you're clumsy, that you're uncoordinated, or that you're going to miss that shot. Someone *who* has already hit it twice. You aren't a *who*—"who is uncoordinated and clumsy" or "a good shot"—but rather you're a *what*—someone shooting a gun.

The Driven D2/D4 person is especially suited for the life of Mastery; in fact, given our wiring, we almost have to get on the path or we will eventually self-sabotage. As Driven, we're wired to feel that it's *never enough* or *not good enough*.

This feeling is what drives us to do amazing things, but it also drives us to shame and to sabotage. The Mastery Mindset doesn't change our drive, but rather directs it. It shifts us from a place of *never enough* or *not good enough* to a mindset where we look for *something more* or *something better*. We realize that we're okay in the present, but that we can be better. This shift is life-changing.

We're able stop trying to cover up our perceived failures, but instead learn to run at them. "How can I be better?" cannot exist if you "didn't screw up," without finding your faults. We're done pretending to be something in the outside world while hiding in an internal "secret, shameful" world. The suffering we experience in our lives stems from the discrepancy between the two worlds. We shift to align the outer and inner world.

Better has no destination and *better* does not mean perfect. This is a huge difference from a mindset that tells us we need to achieve what's on the horizon so we can be okay, or we need to get all A's in college to prove we are smart (and, of course, once we get the A's, we rationalize that anyone could have gotten them because the courses were easy). There is no need for self-hatred, no need for self-sabotage. We shift to a mindset that knows we're okay, but we can always seek to be better. *We can always be better.*

There is excitement in being better, excitement that motivates us to try harder. Better has no finish line. Understanding and believing this is critical to putting an end to self-sabotage.

You may come up with ways to be better but, since better has no finish line, you never failed. You never get there, which is great, because there's no longer a reason to be anxious. With no specific location to run to, there's no reason to rush. There are no more hidden beliefs that "there" is a magical place where all is fine; no more disappointments when we get "there" and still feel as we always have, or as the *who* we've always been. *Who* becomes meaningless. *What* we are is whatever we're doing at this moment in time. It is all that we need focus on. This shift toward being better at *what*ever, not *who*ever we are, is incredibly empowering. By focusing on being better, we can make small, manageable changes that will last our lifetime.

LETTING THE SELF FALL AWAY

The self is constantly changing and constantly evolving. There is no self as you previously understood it—no permanent, fixed entity. When you're with your kids, you're a dad or mom; when you're with your wife, you're a husband; when you're with your employees, you are a boss.

This is so important to us as Driven, as we tend to worry that we're not really what others see, as we struggle with the familiar imposter syndrome and doubt our authenticity. Authenticity is not a feeling, nor is it something you do. Authenticity is a way of being. That authentic way of being is simply allowing yourself to be a teacher or a parent, a friend or an author, or to fully be what you are in that moment.

Remember what we stated earlier: When we ask *who* we are, we see ourselves as a fixed entity with immutable characteristics. When we ask *what* we are, we fully experience ourselves in the moment, as whatever it is we are then.

When we're able to transition, understanding ourselves as *what* we are rather than *who* we are, the inner me and the outer me start to disappear. The monkeys and elephant become integrated. There is no inner world and no outer world. There is only one world.

This is a key component to what presenting styles of meditation are designed to evoke. In this type of meditation, we're practicing to eliminate the difference between the inner world and outer world. When you sense complete presence in the moment, it's called flow. There's the feeling of a cohesive *me* travelling through time, allowing myself to adapt. If you're authentically and fully attempting to teach, you're just a teacher. There is no hidden self, no discrepancy, and no stress that comes from attempting to close the gap between that inner and outer world.

To be a good husband or wife, you must act on the intention to be a better spouse. You have to allow yourself to understand that there is no perfect spouse, and to be genuine in your intention. Knowing better is possible allows us to do that. Self-judgment, self-attacks, and self-criticism have no place in this journey. We must learn to be gentle with ourselves, yet hold ourselves accountable.

It takes tremendous effort to have no effort and just be present. When we experience ourselves in this authentic way, radical transformations can happen quickly. In this decision to stop hiding, to *just* be present in the moment, we find the most satisfaction and contentment. The only thing standing in the way of that contentment is our sense of a fixed or permanent self.

How can we build these new neural networks to replace those that drive us toward self-sabotage? To be successful, we must make one small change at a time. These small changes are the building blocks of new neural pathways, allowing us to subtly, slowly, and smoothly push the upper bandwidth higher and higher. Because we haven't done something radical and abrupt, but rather have made a minor alteration, we are comfortable; we aren't in a completely unfamiliar landscape. Slowly and smoothly, we are doing what is good for ourselves.

Perhaps the greatest challenge lies in identifying a change small enough to be doable. People often underestimate how hard it can be to rewrite longstanding neural pathways. You have to expand the upper end of your bandwidth so that the new area is comfortable, and that takes time and patience.

It is a straightforward process. We make a decision to implement a small change for thirty days. We decide we're not going to eat the whole container of ice cream—we're only going to eat half of it. We live with this for a month. It becomes comfortable. We've moved the bandwidth up just a little. We can tolerate and still manage the change in our CNS without having the elephant go on a subconscious eating rampage. Next month, we eat only a quarter of the container. Months ahead, we switch out the ice cream for an apple. This happens slowly and smoothly. The Driven always roll their eyes at this concept at first. We want it all *now*! This impulse the Driven fall prey to is sabotage in the making. Keeping the change is the most important part of the process. You may judge a small change as "not being enough," but you will be able to keep the change, and it will become part of your new normal paradigm. It will not send the elephants sabotaging impulses in other directions.

We won't always make that good decision and keep the change. We fall off the wagon. When this happens, we judge ourselves. We tend to be harder on ourselves than we would be on anyone else. This judgmental thinking is counterproductive, empowering the monkey mind to write another narrative of *who* you are as a failure. When we get angry, upset, or berate ourselves, we end up moving in the opposite direction of where we want to go. We are back to believing the split between the monkeys and elephant. We lose the logical container.

We need to *gently* come back to making the right decisions and taking the right action. This is the Mastery Mindset. Remember, better has no finish line—there is no ticking clock that is going to run out and result in our losing the race. You are okay in this moment, and you are getting better. You are expanding your bandwidth so you can be content in your new comfort zone. Again, the key is slow, smooth, and fast: We go slow to move smoothly in order to go fast.

This applies whenever we learn something new. Let's say we are learning to shoot a bow and arrow. If we take an arrow and nudge it the correct way, grabbing it with our fingers the correct way, and drawing the bow the correct way—and we do this several times—we are going to begin to build a neural pathway in the brain, an electrical impulse. That electrical impulse in the brain is strengthened every time we repeat the action. It's a physiological phenomenon. That is the basis for the belief that if you really want to learn something, you do it ten thousand times. The neural pathway becomes so strong, it eventually becomes second nature. The elephant can do it without the monkeys' help; the split between them has fallen away.

Once you've built this neural pathway, at a certain point, you won't need that much conscious effort to engage it, using your conscious efforts for other things. You'll have freed up your cognitive skills to think about an ambiguous situation and how to adjust, for example, figuring out the impact of the wind on the arrow. You'll have the cognitive energy to focus on sensing and judging where the target is and where you need to aim and how you're feeling inside. You won't be expending cognitive energy on drawing the bow, or the other basic skills now automatic for you. You'll have built automaticity for the skill. This same automaticity will apply when you are stressed and think to relieve that stress with a brisk walk, rather than a pint of ice cream. It will apply to anything in your life.

In this new Mastery Paradigm, we are free. We have no restrictions on our mind, on our body, or our emotions. It will take time for this to happen. Slow, smooth, then fast.

· CHAPTER 7 ·

STABILIZATION

"Peace comes from within. Do not seek it without."
—THE BUDDHA

Driven are wired to be ready for danger. We're ready for a saber-toothed tiger to pounce on us at any moment. While this has its advantages, as we have discussed, it can also create problems. As Driven, our elephant is typically loaded with fear and our monkeys jabber away, coming up with all kinds of emotional connections, directions, and decisions, all founded on the existence of this saber-tooth tiger. If we expect that saber-tooth everywhere, we may see it in a harmless house cat.

Being able to calm the elephant down—often the most challenging task for the Driven—is critical to seeing past our biases to the real world. A stable CNS enables us to recognize that the tiger is just a cat; it gives us a better look at reality. As such, we can make better decisions and get us where we want to go.

The key to a more stable CNS is becoming familiar with the sensations in the elephant (interoception), to know and work within our bandwidth, and ultimately to expand it. Remember, as the elephant gets pinged and the monkey mind confirms its validity, we will only look for things to further confirm the ping, and then the biases become stronger. This can set into motion a self-fulfilling prophecy. If this cycle continues and the elephant is increasingly dys-regulated, we will hit the edge of our bandwidth and the monkeys and elephant will fight for control. Here, we turn ropes into snakes, miss opportunities and, worse, we turn snakes into ropes, leading to sabotage. However, when the elephant is in a safe environment and the monkeys are paying attention to the present, the parasympathetic takes over and calms us down.

So, how do we get out of the way and let the elephant calm down? How do we stabilize? *Getting* stabilized requires a divorce between you and your action. By "divorce," we mean disconnecting from any and all action long enough to allow our reactive subconscious selves to stop living on autopilot. This requires the logical container—the means of strictly observing from a place of curiosity, without judging or acting. You must acknowledge the logical truth that right now, in the present, nothing is wrong—neither in your mind, nor in your body.

There is an old saying in meditation practice that states, "It takes tremendous effort to have no effort." This could not be truer. Not doing anything is actually very difficult and takes practice.

Initially, the calming you achieve may be short-lived and vary greatly, depending on the situation you are in. Over time though, it will get easier—the logical container will fall away, and this will become your natural reaction to sensations in the body.

When you use the Driven Meditation (DM) style of breathing and your eyes to scan the outer world, it is not as difficult to land in the present moment as you may think. The logical truth that right now nothing is wrong, we are relatively safe, applies to nearly all of the moments of our entire life. Eventually, you may find a growing sense of peace in many situations that used to shake you up. If this sounds like faith, you're right. (We will explore spirituality in later chapters.) The safe reality of the moment will start to sink into the elephant, and the monkeys will quiet down. Fortunately, our CNS and biology work in our favor to meet this challenge. For those of us wired to never quit or die trying, for those of us who like a challenge, this is an ideal task—a task we're equal to.

While getting stabilized is a divorce from your actions, *being* stabilized is a blending of you, your body, and your actions. It occurs when you have the clarity to experience the intention in your body and the actions coming from a heartfelt place, not as a subconscious reaction. The logical container then begins to *fall away*, and we start to experience ourselves as a fluid expression of our intention. (This will be explored in greater detail in the chapter on manifestation.)

YOUR BEGINNER'S MIND: MEDITATION AS A LEARNING TOOL

We now understand the importance of being able to catch the elephant's impulses that drive our self-sabotaging behavior. But how do we hone our abilities to do that?

The first thing to keep in mind is that no one will teach you how. There are now over seven billion human CNSs on this planet and every one of them is different. There are obviously many similarities among us humans, but we are all essentially unique. There isn't a one-size-fits-all formula handed down with exact details for how to rewire your body and mind. For instruction to truly fit you and your needs, you must become your own teacher. You do this by becoming a better student of your body.

There is a very old foundational principle in Mastery that states, "Have No Guru." It means that you never want to idolize a teacher. Idolization creates biases that potentially distort what you hear and limit your ability to learn. Blind faith in a teacher stifles curiosity. You believe you have heard the "final word" from this sage, so you are less likely to inquire further, less likely to stop and analyze. The Buddha was expressly clear on this point. He repeatedly stated he was just a normal man and not a Messiah figure. Even in Christianity, Christ taught that he was brought as an example of how to act and behave, not be held as an idol. In fact, much of why society rejected him as the Messiah was because he refused to become a political leader and idol, and he rebelled against the political oppression happening at the time. He portrayed himself to be a personal Messiah, saving his followers from an inner world of oppression rather than becoming an outer world leader. If you so choose to believe *and experience* an embodiment of Christ, you must take *in* his nature and feel internal peace, not hold Christ as an external idol that gives you the answer for your life. You do not want to get caught up in someone else's solution for your life. You don't want to be closed off because you believe blindly in a teacher. You want to be open to a possibility that your internal experience holds a pearl of wisdom beyond price. You want to find your own true nature and find peace and faith within. An old Kabbalah saying can be paraphrased as, "If you want to disappoint Yah [self-existing one or God, the great mystery of God], seek him. He's not lost or disconnected from you, you're the one who's lost and disconnected from Yah." You are not separate from the earth.

In Japanese schools of meditation, this type of mindset is a self-learning openness called, "the beginner's mind." In the beginner's mind, there are limitless possibilities; in the expert's mind, there exists only a few. The beginner's mind means you will question; it means you will be curious; it means you will be open-minded.

As Driven, we are naturally skeptical, but this skepticism can actually be an asset when learning, provided we avoid the negative bias and assumption that often accompanies it. Nothing slows your ability to take in new information than a healthy dose of judgment and a preconceived idea of what is right. The ones who learn are the ones who are receptive to new information from the perspective of healthy curiosity and skepticism. In other words, they don't buy into anything without being curious and without questioning, but they don't close the door either. The ones who make the most progress keep an open mind.

WHAT IS MEDITATION?

To calm our elephant, we need to get into the present moment where it feels safe. We need to catch those impulses telling us something is wrong, so our decisions are based on reality; we don't want to be running on autopilot and reacting to our inner world. One of the best ways to learn this is to integrate a six-hundred-year-old presenting style of meditation practice into your day-to-day life.

Meditation has been around for thousands of years and is practiced in just about all societies. People have a broad base of associations with the word meditation and you may be familiar with some of them. They share some similarities, but are different enough to make them specific tools for specific purposes.

Most meditation techniques are not presenting practices. Rather, they are relaxation training or in some cases, spiritual training. These techniques may be of great value if relaxation or spiritual training is the goal, but again, they aren't the right tool for the Driven to calm the elephant.

Some meditation techniques may actually be ill-advised for the Driven, pushing us outside of our bandwidth. Such approaches may create very blissful numbed-out states in the body, truly sensational, but they are completely going in the wrong direction for stability. We become dissociated from reality, stuck riding the blissful sensations. This is the opposite of being connected and will sabotage your life.

Before we go any further, let's look at some of the best-known meditation techniques. We want to be on the same page about what we mean when we talk about meditation for the Driven. The following techniques are *not* what we mean.

Contemplation, a very popular style of meditation, involves thinking about a subject, a process, a thought, a truth, a perception. You focus on an idea and notice the sensations created in the body. This deepens your experience of truth so you can extract something important and valuable for you.

Contemplative meditation is like a cognitive digestion process. You chew on the ideas, have the experience in the body, and incorporate it into your life. Many people, when they think about meditation, especially in the context of religious traditions, think of this contemplative exercise. Prayer may fall into this category. Although it can be an interesting cognitive and physical experience, contemplative meditation does not align with our objectives; it does not bring us into the safe present.

Insight meditation, or Vipassana, is an inner journey

through which we examine what we are, how we are, and what's happening inside of us. Popular in India, this type of meditation eventually took root in China and was instrumental in the birth of Buddhism and many types of yogic traditions. Other religious traditions also use this type of meditation.

Most meditative traditions draw on insight meditation. Insight meditation can be risky for the Driven. Some of the techniques are intended to split the elephant into smaller and smaller sensations. This may seem to diminish anxiety and CNS dysregulation almost immediately, but these approaches do not stabilize the whole elephant by connecting the elephant to the outer world in a natural, biologically congruent way. We do not want to get lost in our bodily sensations if we want to stabilize.

Some meditation practices serve to distort reality. Transcendental meditation, for example, is literally designed to transcend this reality. This is also risky for Driven types who may be drawn toward the wonderful sensations created in the body. As stated earlier, getting lost in your inner world of bliss means getting further from feeling safe in reality.

Still other types of meditations are used as a way of reprogramming your mind. Neuro-linguistic programming draws on some of the techniques used in hypnosis to change beliefs or reactions. Motivational speakers draw on techniques to change people's reality.

Reality distortion is typically not what we want when we're beginning to understand ourselves as human beings. It often moves us away from that path. That being said, there's a time and a place where reality distortion is appropriate. Consider a natural introvert going to a party that is very important to his business. He has to be outgoing, despite social interaction being completely outside of his comfort zone. He might concentrate for a little bit, thinking and visualizing every person in the room is his friend. He is neuro-linguistic programming his mind to be able to be sociable at the party; thus, he is preparing himself for success.

We see this type of meditation applied in the armed forces as well. When young men join the Marine Corps, they are, to some extent, brainwashed. Neuro-linguistic programming turns men into warriors, whether or not they were actually born that way. The monkeys are all trained in concert with each other to believe in the new reality, a reality that has been distorted so that they can go to war and fight.

Although few people want a war, there is sometimes a

need for one, just as there are other circumstances when fears are overtaking you and reality distortion can help you do what you need to do. It's very common. You've probably heard the old expression, "Fake it 'til you make it." This is definitely not what we're talking about when we talk about meditation as a way to stabilize your CNS.

Unfortunately, people don't always use meditation appropriately. They don't identify the right form of meditation for their needs, using different forms of meditation interchangeably believing there are many ways to climb a mountain. This is not the case. When we are sick, we must identify the medication that addresses our particular illness if we're going to get better. Meditation is no different—we need to select the one that maps to our goals. For the Driven, the goal is to address the monkey/ elephant split and stabilize the CNS so we can get a better look at reality.

DRIVEN MEDITATION [DM]

Driven Meditation or DM (based on the Japanese meditation Zazen) is uniquely suited to the needs of the Driven. The purpose of this type of meditation is to practice *being* in the present, connect with the now, and *gently* come back to experiencing the present when our monkey mind wanders. We're building a skill that makes us more effective, strengthens us mentally and spiritually, and brings emotional balance to our daily lives. When practiced with the right attitude and technique, we experience the benefits immediately.

Your breathing style and posture are critical to maximizing the return on investment and to experiencing the immediate benefits from your meditation.

You can meditate on any comfortable cushion. Although there are specialized cushions (zafu and zabuton) for meditation, they are not necessary. However, having them set out in a conspicuous location, especially if you need to step over them, can be a useful trigger to help you get on the cushion daily. If you prefer, you can sit on a stiff pillow or rolled up blanket. In fact, any upright, stiff-backed chair works, so you have no excuse for not meditating while traveling.

SITTING ON A CHAIR

The correct posture for sitting in a chair is important for aligning your body structure upright. Proper posture allows for the free flow of information between head and body, building interoception. It also allows us to let go of conscious muscle control and rely on the body's subconscious support muscles. Letting go of control is one of the greatest challenges and benefits of DM practice. The monkeys do not need to control the elephant; this belief is the *split* between them. By letting go of control of the elephant, we build faith that the body is safe and can manage itself. Eventually, the illusion of this split will fall away, for moments, at first. Then, your capacity for sitting in a parasympathetic state will increase. This is often experienced as spiritual feelings of deep faith and contentment. Perfect faith does not come easily, but then again, why should it? This is a challenge worthy of the Driven.

To support the proper alignment, it's essential that the chair have a somewhat stiff, flat seat. Too soft of a cushion makes the proper body posture difficult to achieve. Begin by placing your feet flat on the floor with uncrossed legs. A small cushion or folded hand towel under the back half of the buttocks encourages a soft, natural curve in the lumbar area of the spine. The top of the pelvic bone should be parallel to the floor with the knees slightly below the hips. It should feel as if you are sitting at a slight forward tilt. Straighten your spine above the lumbar as if a string is lifting you through the top of your head and providing support.

The three traditional seated positions are kneeling (*seiza*), cross-legged with feet on thighs (half or full lotus), and cross-legged with feet on the ground (Burmese). You may find that one position fits your body type more than another. Being comfortable is key. If you are new to meditation, find a teacher who can set you up in the right posture and try the different postures. You can visit our website at http://highlydriven.life or search the internet for pictures of these positions.

KNEELING (SEIZA)

For the *Seiza* position, kneel and place a stiff pillow (or *zafu* or *seiza* stool) between your legs and rest on the bones of your buttocks, with the tailbone centered towards the front of the cushion like you are sitting on a horse. The cushion must be high enough and stiff enough to keep your legs from falling asleep and your ankles relatively pain-free. Most of your weight should be on your buttocks, with only modest pressure on your knees resting on a blanket or soft flat cushion on the ground. Straighten your spine as if there is a string running from your body through the top of your head lifting you and providing support. You want a soft, natural curve in the lumbar area of the spine. Keep the top of the pelvic bone parallel to the floor by sitting forward on the cushion, allowing a slight forward tilt.

CROSS-LEGGED WITH FEET ON THE THIGHS (LOTUS)

Sitting with your legs crossed and with the ability to bring your feet to your thighs (lotus position) requires some degree of flexibility. You may try a half-Lotus or, if you are very flexible, a full Lotus position. For a half-Lotus, sit on the forward edge of the cushion and bring your right foot on top of your left thigh. Leave your left foot relaxed under your right thigh, resting on the ground. For the full Lotus, bring your left foot on top of your right thigh to form a pretzel shape. Make sure both knees are on the ground and your tailbone is comfortably on the front edge of the cushion to create a proper tilt to the pelvis.

CROSS-LEGGED WITH FEET ON THE GROUND (BURMESE)

Similar to the Lotus, the Burmese position opens up your hips while you bring your right foot to your left calf, and your left foot to your right calf. Both ankles and knees are on the ground, making for a great deal of stability. If both knees cannot be in complete contact with the floor, do not sit in the cross-legged position. It is impossible to achieve correct posture unless both knees are on the ground forming a triangle of support with both knees and buttocks.

SETTLING IN

Once you are seated in any of the above positions, begin moving front-to-back and side-to-side a little bit to settle into a naturally upright, straight position with the center of gravity in the pelvic cradle. Relax your face, neck, shoulders, chest, and back muscles, trusting the core abdominal muscles to naturally find the center of gravity. You may notice a small, seemingly subconscious circular oscillation of fluid movement from the base of the spine. You are becoming conscious of a subconscious parasympathetic vestibular function that maintains centered upright balance. This subtle movement is strong evidence that you have achieved the correct posture.

Remember, the objective of this type of meditation is not to relax or to get caught up with the sensations going on in the body. We are trying to connect to reality and the present moment. Since the present moment is safe, relaxation is a bi-product of this practice.

HANDS, HEAD, AND EYES

Your hands, head, and eyes have specific positions. Your hands can be placed in one of two positions: Either palms down and comfortably relaxed on the top of the thighs, or in a circle known as a mudra. To form a mudra, rest your dominant hand about two-to-three inches, palm up, below your navel, and place your other hand on top of it. To form the circle, let the thumbs lightly touch. Keep the hands very close and in contact with the body with the top of the thumbs slightly below the navel.

Head position is extremely important. Keep your head upright without tilting it to either side, as if you are looking straightforward. Bring your head slightly back, tucking your chin to keep your ears centered over your shoulders. It is very important to keep your chin and jawline parallel with the top of the pelvis. Both should be parallel with the floor.

Most people hold lots of tension in their head, neck, and jaw, so there's a tendency for the head to shift forward during meditation. To avoid shifting your head, visualize the center of your skull base sitting on top of and centered on the spinal column; this should create a very slight curve in the neck similar to a healthy lumbar curve. Your ears should be equidistant from the spine and centered over the shoulders. You may pull your head back slightly to center your ears over your shoulders and your shoulders over your hips.

Many people new to this posture report a sensation as if they are falling back. This is to be expected and is part of the process of learning to let go. You are learning to trust the subconscious support muscles in the back and core, while learning to trust and have faith that your body will support you.

Driven Meditation (DM) requires that the eyes be open. Driven are visually dominant. As you have learned, we use our eyes to make sense of the world and watch for the threat that may be around any corner. Seventy percent of our neocortex is dedicated to eyesight. If we close our eyes, we are giving up our dominant safety detector, while also freeing our multi-thinking to go wild, which makes being in the present much more difficult. We also want to take advantage of the fact that everything we see is always happening in the present moment.

Your eyes should be partially open, described as softly open rather than wide open. Eventually, you will want to drop your gaze to a forty-five-degree downward angle to a spot about one meter in front of you. You can place a candle there or just focus on a spot on the ground. Be very conscious to keep your head straight forward and not drop your chin as you bring your eyes down; keep the chin, shoulders, and pelvis parallel to the floor. This lowered gaze can be awkward or even very unsettling at first. You may experience neck and shoulder tension. Gently work toward this forty-five-degree downward gaze over time; it may take years. You don't want to close your eyes or force your gaze down.

Experimenting with the degree to which you can "comfortably" drop your eyes can help you to find the center and edges of your bandwidth. This can be extremely helpful in understanding the subtlest pings of guardedness in the elephant and will build your capacity to not react to the pings. Your eyesight is one of the primary ways you keep your world safe. For the Driven, to be on guard is normal. With your head position level with your hips, both parallel to the ground, looking forward is the quickest way to detect threat in your immediate environment. This keeps those ready for threat safe.

In working with active and retired SEAL Team guys, we have found that changing this threat orientation can raise the arousal level quickly. For the Driven, it is scary to give up control and not be on guard. We all lack faith but, for the Driven, dropping our guard is extremely difficult. The elephant doesn't like not being ready for a threat by dropping the gaze towards the ground, while keeping the head parallel with the ground.

Finding the edge of the "threat" radar ping in the elephant, when the eyes just begin to drop, helps build interoception and finds the smallest edge of the bandwidth moving away from the "normal" guarded center point. Play with this. Look forward and find the proper head and body position, and then very slowly drop your gaze. Often, the elephant ping will feel like a slight tightening in the diaphragm, and you'll experience increased difficulty letting the breath go. Move the gaze slightly up and find the place where the body lets go of this tension. Then, breathing becomes more comfortable again. This is the internal awareness of our bandwidth we are going for. Gently move the gaze lower again, slowly, and feel the elephant just begin to go on guard. Gently hold the gaze in this spot, catch the monkey mind and the elephant impulse to change the gaze. Logically contain this experience by knowing that the actual threat level has not increased. Have faith that you are safe. Usually after a minute or two, the elephant's initial ping and tightening will begin to soften, and the body tension will slowly dissipate. You may feel an overall body sensation of expansion, and you may feel a greater desire for a deep full breath. *Take it!* You have just increased your bandwidth and tolerance of being safe in the present. This is the practice of DM and rewiring the body to be more tolerant. It will take years to fully let your guard go and have complete and perfect faith, even for just a moment or two. Mastery of the CNS is never-ending; there is no finish line. Be patient, curious, and steadfast.

BREATHING

The breathing technique used in DM is possibly the most

distinctive feature, differentiating it from other forms of meditation. If performed correctly, people are likely to see immediate benefits. This style of breathing is a powerful way to kick in the parasympathetic and increase your Heart Rate Variability (HRV), which have a profound, positive impact on the health of mind and body.

Closely following the posture recommendations, begin the breathing technique by keeping your mouth gently closed with teeth lightly touching without clenching your jaw. A slight chattering of the teeth is often reported. This is normal. Gently relax the jaw and move the head position to tuck in the chin. An impulse to close the jaw more tightly to stop the chattering is also often reported. Don't follow this impulse. Gently open the jaw to make space between the teeth. The chattering may increase but will slow over time. Place your tongue on the roof of your mouth. Breathe silently and gently through your nose. Ideally, the only muscles you'll use to move the breath in and out are the lower abdominal muscles below the navel (if in a mudra, behind your hands) and the muscles of the pelvic floor.

It is very important to completely relax the face, jaw, neck, shoulders, chest, and back muscles as much as possible. The only tension in the body should be in the lower abdomen below the navel and the deep core muscle of the pelvis. If everything else is relaxed, increasing tension in this area gently "lifts" the diaphragm by compressing the organs up toward the chest, gently expanding the lungs and chest on the *in* breath.

Take a soft but full breath. Then slowly (at least a count of ten) and consciously relax the tension in the lower abdominals and pelvic floor, allowing the belly to slowly soften. You should feel the sensation that gravity is taking the breath effortlessly from the body, an indicator of a correct breathing technique. Do not "push" the breath out with any muscle tension.

People often describe breathing in DM as "reverse" breathing. You may feel as if the breath is rising from deep within the body, coming up to the top of the head when you breathe in, and then dropping back down slowly as you breathe out. It is very important that you use only minimal effort to take in a breath, and that you surrender effort on the outbreath. This is the way to be in control of giving up control of the elephant. "I" inhale and "I" disappear on the exhalation.

The rhythms of inhalation vary, but you will spend about one-third of the time slowly inhaling and two-thirds of the time on exhale. You may experience a longer and longer pause at the bottom of the breath. Most people report a sensation of vasodilation (sense that the body is expanding/softening or the Chi is grounding through the pelvic floor) and increased relaxation is on the exhalation. The pause at the bottom of the breath may seem to be quite long at times, but when you feel the elephant's impulse to breathe, follow this impulse and begin the inhalation. At the bottom of the breath, there is often an increase in the subtle circular oscillation sensation of the muscles. This is a sign that the elephant is starting to be in charge. Your tolerance for maintaining stable parasympathetic relaxation is the Mastery Path.

CONCENTRATION AND FOCUS OF ATTENTION

Those with visual-dominant brains benefit from a technique that pairs eyesight with breathing. Following these steps leads to two very powerful abilities—hyperfocus and hypofocus.

To develop hyperfocus, during inhalation, focus your gaze with some intensity on a single point on the ground or on the very tip of the candle. Seeing the object of your attention with an increasing sharpness and clarity, sometimes to an extraordinary level, indicates that you are using the correct intensity of focus.

This new level of awareness may encourage your analysis

of the object. You may also experience this point of focus, your breath, and your body as the only objects that exist. It is very important that you don't attempt to tune anything out as you focus. Rather, your increased concentration on this single point and your controlled breath should naturally hold your focus.

To develop hypofocus, on the exhalation, begin to release your effort on the point of focus but maintain the center of your gaze on the same spot. With an ever-increasing surrender of effort of both sight and breath, curiously notice everything in your periphery without moving your eyes. Typically, all the senses become heightened to great detail during the exhalation. Notice the air on the skin, the sounds around you, the internal body sensations, anything and everything that is happening in the present. This hypofocus is often experienced as a blended connection of mind, body, and the world. The subject and object awareness of hyperfocus seems to *fall away* and you may feel as if you and the environment have become one.

The hypo/hyperfocus practices are anchors to the present. Your mental and sensory attention should be just on the present moment—the goal for the Driven. The ability to alternate between hypo/hyperfocus is a powerful tool and is amazing fuel for the mind of the Driven. The application of this skill is very powerful in daily life.

BEING GENTLE WITH THE "SELF" AND THE WANDERING MIND

As you develop your abilities, you may need to remind yourself to return to your point of focus. Your approach will be gentle, lighthearted, and fueled by curiosity. Maintaining an open curiosity of the point of focus is key.

Your mind will wander and break your concentration on the present. Through DM, you'll be able to quickly catch the monkey mind and bring focus back to the experiences of the here and now. This can be a frustrating experience for anyone attempting to meditate for the first time. We all have some very mean monkeys living in our heads. We soon discover our inner judging critic begins to attack us. This is expected. It cannot be emphasized enough that you must learn to meet this critic with laughter and curiosity, rather than with more effort.

Less effort is essential to gaining the neurological benefits from DM. For the Driven person, it is often hardest to ease up and not force efforts. Once you understand, "It takes tremendous effort to have no effort," then, you begin to appreciate the true challenge behind not quitting meditation as a Driven.

Unlike many of the challenges that Driven thrive on, this particular challenge does not involve a grade to earn, a mountain to climb, a race to run, a company to develop, or a product to invent. The challenge is to be kind to ourselves. Perhaps the best way to understand this concept is to envision a Labrador puppy who is being trained to be a service dog. You tell him to sit and you gently push his butt to the ground, but he's going to get up and walk away because he's a puppy. You're not going to berate the pup, because he doesn't fully understand. Rather, you'll gently bring him back, sit him down, and do it again and again and again. Eventually, sooner than you think, he learns to sit. Then he'll learn to stay, and then to lie down. You'll have a well-trained puppy. Eventually, he'll develop the skills he needs to be a badass service dog.

We want our minds to be like the service dog. We don't want to be beholden to a mind no different from the undisciplined puppy. However, that well-trained service dog was once the undisciplined puppy. He becomes the animal that can be trusted to aid disabled people through patient training, not through anger and not through beatings. When we correct a dog, we don't beat him. Beating a dog doesn't work and takes his training in the wrong direction.

While we agree that we would not beat a dog, we beat ourselves all the time—we beat our minds with self-judgments. We call ourselves *stupid* or *sorry*. It hurts us more than it helps. The self-judgment keeps us destabilized. When we judge ourselves, we just upset ourselves, and we get no closer to the goal. If anything, we move further from it.

This unnecessary internal stress has been repeatedly demonstrated to decrease efficiency, reduce mental clarity, and increase the likelihood of poor decision-making. This stress affects your leadership skills, relationships, and overall well-being. It leads to a host of physical problems from heart disease to bad skin. By learning to laugh at oneself and lighten up, you impart permanent neurological changes that increase efficiency, productivity, and overall life satisfaction. This may take years of practice, but you will get better at this and, as you know, better has no finish line.

PERSONAL ACCOUNTABILITY AND KEEPING A DAILY PRACTICE

As Driven people, it's in our nature to overestimate what we can do in a day. We want to climb a mountain, build a house, change the course of a company, or learn a new skill in that one day. We need to remember that learning doesn't happen all at once, or in a single day. It takes time, day after day, and year after year.

You want to begin with two minutes of DM a day for the first week, preferably in the same place and at the same time. You need to make a commitment to put it into your morning routine. Meditation first thing in the morning or very close to first thing is important. Our cortisol stress hormones are highest in the morning, and that's when we receive the greatest benefit from going off autopilot. If you practice other types of meditation, then put the two minutes of DM at the end of those practices, as a separate practice.

Getting to the cushion on a daily basis is harder than it sounds, but it is critical. This daily practice is one of the life-changing lessons of meditation and the best way to develop true personal accountability—the kind of accountability that matters most, which is when nobody's watching.

You may have opportunities to watch the elephant and the monkeys fighting with one another as the monkeys prod the elephant to meditate, or colluding with one another and generating an excuse to skip DM. Catch yourself making a mental story that supports why this incredibly simple, two-minute task is too difficult or "not worth doing."

Don't get caught up in the fight between an angry "drive" to push through the "resistance" or a submissive internal excuse-maker. Once you can experience the embodied resistance of the elephant before it becomes mental chatter, your life will begin to change, sometimes dramatically. If you can become curious about the resistance, if you can question it, and then laugh about it rather than assuming the resistance is valid, you will realize even more benefits. You will develop a greater ability to be present and just sit down to meditate. Before you know it, you may begin to recognize and experience that resistance does not exist in the present. No resistance. No forcing. Just doing. This is the greatest benefit of a daily DM practice. The experience of letting the resistance toward a future activity physically fall away is often an extremely liberating experience. This skill quickly spills into every activity in your daily life, from returning emails to completing that dissertation to repairing the drywall in the basement. We are free to do anything in this life without any resistance.

Once you meditate daily for one week, increase the time by only two minutes the next week. Slowly step up the time commitment each week until you get to twenty minutes every morning. Life does get in the way sometimes and on some mornings, time constraints may make DM seemingly impossible. Yet, there is never a valid excuse for not sitting down for just a minute or doing even just a few DM breaths. Getting to the cushion is half the battle and much of the benefit. There is never a valid excuse.

This is a path with some amazing insights along the way.

The effort is minimal and the return is phenomenal. The challenge is not easy. It's truly an extreme sport for the highly Driven, without a finish line because, as any Driven person will tell you, better has no finish line.

GETTING STABLE ENOUGH

At first, getting stabilized can feel clunky and make you think you're getting worse. We often hear from new clients in the first few months that we are making them worse, especially if they are doing DM daily. Usually, it sounds like, "Holy shit, I'm an anxious mess all the time!" Research repeatedly supports that a consistent meditation practice increases reports of anxiety. These findings are probably why many more people start a meditation practice but don't maintain the practice. Why would anyone want to be more anxious?

The truth is, they're not. What's happening is that you are becoming more aware that your inner world is a less accurate reflection of the real world around you. When you experience this awareness, and stop creating a story to explain why you are more anxious, that's when you'll know the meditation is working correctly, and you are becoming stabilized. It sounds circular, but being able to recognize your instability increases your stability. Building body awareness and increasing interoception helps you understand where you're operating in the bandwidth continuum. The internal arousal thermometer sensitivity is going up and we can catch it quicker as it shifts.

Meditation increases awareness of anxiety but lowers actual arousal. You may find that things that only functioned as radar pings, and went unnoticed, now come into your awareness. This is progress. We are becoming more aware of our subconscious influence on perceptions, emotions, decisions we make, and the subtle impulses in the body. This is what the expression "expanding your consciousness" means. We are waking up to the world outside of our biases and perceptions.

The key skill in stability is the curiosity and recognition of how close to "losing it" you are. You begin to understand how your emotions are changing your perceptions of reality. If you stick with your DM, you will soon find situations going more smoothly. Your effort to keep it together will no longer be an issue.

BEING STABLE ENOUGH

We all have circumstances where we feel comfortable, calm, clear, and on top of everything, but we tend to pay attention to the situations that make us anxious and move us to the negative end of our bandwidth. Driven are wired to focus on that negative end; it is much harder for us to bring to mind those more comfortable times.

To move from *getting* stable to *being* stable, we must become familiar with the sensations that tell us we're okay. The practice of noticing when your CNS is stable and what this is like in your body is critical to making the transition. As Driven, we're used to working to keep it together, even if we aren't consciously aware of the feelings. We want to shift our mindset and recognize that we're okay—for this to be our new normal.

Feeling okay enables us to catch a ping to our radar much more quickly. Once we detect the ping, we can use the logical container to do some reality testing: You note the ping, then you assess what your elephant is telling you and what is really happening. In order to calm your elephant so this is possible, you must learn not to judge those sensations in your body. Rather, you must approach them with curiosity.

At first, this takes conscious effort—sometimes a great deal of effort. Soon, this process will become reflexive and being stable will become the norm. It will no longer take conscious effort to be in balance; it will come naturally.

MEDITATION FOR LIFE

Randy recounts one example that really illustrates the power of stabilization. We were at the range for an advanced three-day DM shooting retreat not too long ago. It was very hot, ninety-five degrees on the range, probably one of the hottest days we'd had in a long time. One of the guys in the group was intensely upset about the heat.

"It's hot," he complained.

"It's hot," I agreed.

"Yes," he grumbled.

"Are you sweating?" I asked.

"Yes," he replied, clearly annoyed.

"How do you feel the heat?" I questioned.

"Well, I feel it in my hands and in my head."

"Okay. Is that good or bad?"

He says, "It's bad."

"Really?" I replied with a snicker.

He caught himself as soon as he said the word "bad." He recognized that he was judging reality and assigning a value to the temperature. When you judge reality, you are taken out of the present because you wish you were in the future where you would be comfortable in an air-conditioned space. He was someone *who* was hot, and wished he was someone *who* could be cool. He lost the reality of *what* he was doing. As a SEAL, you learn that hot and cold feelings are just that—hot and cold. It's our reaction that creates the problem, not the temperatures themselves.

Until the temperature gets to the point that is damaging to your health, the temperature is just a question of comfort. When you internalize that the heat does not impact what you are doing, you stay in the present. You no longer have the resistance generated by focusing on the way things "should be" in the future.

The guy on the range was caught in the desire to be in an air-conditioned room. His focus on that future prevented him from being in the present. While you can acknowledge that it would be nice to be in an air-conditioned room, you need to bring yourself back to the present, reminding yourself that right now you must live with the heat.

As highly Driven people, we want to fix everything; that

is a natural and preferred characteristic for us. We aren't suggesting you ignore or discount your desire to improve things. We never want to change our Driven gifts. What we want is to balance that ambition with the objective of living in the present. We need to recognize that there's a time and place for improving a situation, and that this ambition will not be self-sabotaging at that time and place. There wouldn't be inventions if people didn't aspire to make things better. How we try to change for the better is what makes the difference.

People who focus on how hot and miserable they are will more likely sabotage themselves. Those who accept that they are hot and are willing to wait can take on the challenge. Consider inventors. They are never held back by what "should" work, but by what isn't working. Rather than stubbornly sticking with a plan, they accept when an approach isn't working. They move on and try something else. They don't let the fantasy of what "should be" run their lives.

Retraining your brain does not come easily. If it did, most of the Driven would grow bored with the process. DM is challenging, more than any other form of meditation, and potentially more than anything you've ever attempted. The work, however, aligns with your needs as a Driven.

We have nothing against guided "meditation," or

medicinal or some recreational substances to escape from your reality. You should be aware of what you are doing though—that you are escaping from a personally biased reality that probably does not exist. These practices do nothing to improve your ability to move through the real world. These meditations and drugs may make it much harder for you in the long run, and move you away from where you want to be.

What helps the Driven is embodying specific ways of increasing your bandwidth of CNS arousal without causing outbursts of fear. This is exactly what Basic Underwater Demolition/SEAL (BUD/S) training is about. Our objective in increasing our bandwidth is to decrease the likelihood of fear-driven impulses, which hinder your success.

Ultimately, we want to create *optimal flow states*—states in which we are completely present in what we are doing. To achieve these flow states, we must first tune down the CNS into parasympathetic stability, and then gradually turn it up while remaining connected to our surroundings.

We may look like workaholic Type A's because our tolerance and need for stress is different. In fact, the Driven require a certain amount of stress to generate their dopamine. We may also be drawn to hyperfocused situations that trigger our NPY to induce flow. Interoception provides an awareness of our bodies to find that stress level sweet spot for optimal performance, at our choosing. If you're bouncing from one end of your bandwidth to the other, you won't be stable enough to assess your ideal stress levels. You'll be, in a sense, working with questionably reliable information about reality.

Our long-term goal as Driven D2/D4s is to learn to be okay with reality as we sense it—to respond to the world around us and within us without reacting impulsively. In this way, we stabilize both our internal world and our lives, not battling either. The highly Driven superhero knows that becoming a Master starts with looking inside. Once we open the Pandora's Box of our mind's reality and check it against the real world, we can stabilize. True meditation empowers us to passively observe without fighting our impulses. True meditation is not about trying to feel good, relax, or do anything at all.

For a Driven to learn to sit and do nothing is incredibly challenging, but we have the no-quit attitude that enables us to meet this incredible challenge. It takes a tremendous amount of effort to truly embrace these teachings, but the outcome of feeling safe in the present while never satisfied with the future unlocks our true potential.

· CHAPTER 8 ·

GETTING ORGANIZED

"In the beginner's mind, there are many possibilities, in the expert's mind, there are few."
—SHUNRYU SUZUKI

Japanese swords are known to be some of the world's best. Handmade even today in an extremely intricate process, these swords do not break in battle. The swordmaker puts hard metal on top of soft metal and folds it again, and again, and again, thousands of times. Hard metal will break and soft metal will bend; yet, when you fold them together over and over, you're taking the best attributes of each metal and turning them into the most exquisite cutting machine in the world. These swords don't easily lose their edge, and they're curved at exactly the right angle.

Just as we'd craft a sword in a certain organized way, we do much the same thing with our minds and bodies. We must be soft and gentle in attitude, but strong and accountable in action. We take the best attributes of our gifts—our left brain, which is analytical and story-driven; our right brain, which is emotional and creative; and our body, which has the ability to act instinctively—and blend them harmoniously. Through our DM practice, which we build into every aspect of our daily lives, we develop the skills to integrate all parts of our body-mind into one whole experience. The ability to experience and integrate the impulsive, the emotional, and the logical parts of our life as a whole results in a flow—that fluid state in which we perform at our optimal best.

BLENDING THE SELVES INTO EVERY ACTION

There's an old Japanese saying that states, "When chopping wood, just chop wood. When carrying water, just carry water." Today, we say, "When answering email, just answer email." When any task is done in the present—with our logical and emotional brains and body aligned as one whole, just doing the task—the process is fluid, effective, and efficient.

When we organize the internal process, we meld the brain and body together; they become fluid and nearly indistinguishable, just as the metals in the Japanese sword when folded repeatedly. Before we can achieve that fluidity in ourselves, we must separate the parts and understand them. Then we can create a process that allows the typically dominate, logical brain to become secondary and just another part of the whole experience.

We (Doug and Randy) have identified specific activities, such as long-range shooting, martial arts, throwing darts, and putting golf balls, to create concrete experiences of how we integrate the mind and body as we move through life. The principles learned in these activities apply to a broad base of contexts.

To be successful at any of these activities, you must eliminate the split between the monkey mind and the subconscious elephant, and the sabotage that is likely to follow that split. You must be in the present where everything is okay.

Consider what it means to shoot a gun. To shoot well, we have to think about how to hold the gun, how to pull the trigger, and the calculations we need to adjust for the wind. The same type of thinking is required for martial arts. We learn how to move out of the way of a strike, how to block, how to start a grappling sequence, and what that sequence should be. You must be in the present to do this.

The process of throwing a dart is incredibly simple, but it can create extreme focus. Putting, in golf, is perhaps the simplest skill to learn, but the hardest to truly master.

Interestingly, although you've heard that to perfect a skill you need to perform it ten thousand times, the reality is we only need to do it a few times if we're fully present during that practice. If we clearly understand the process, and we are present at every moment, we learn quickly. We can learn long-range shooting in a day. We can take a novice and teach him to do what even most SEAL snipers take weeks to learn.

The first step to integrating meditation in every action begins with the cognitive process of going through the procedure within your left, or logical brain. The logical brain is responsible for the principles—the analytical piece—of learning the steps. For shooting, those are how to mount the gun to the shoulder, load the gun, adjust for wind, hold the gun, and adjust the scope.

The second step may include some creativity and emotional or intentional purpose; it is the emotional brain's connection to the activity. The emotional brain focuses on the feeling of the experience, the sensory components, and the emotional involvement. How does it feel when I do this? What is the feel of pulling the trigger? What is the temperature of the trigger? What does it smell like? How do I get a little creative? You may recognize the emotional brain's contribution and connection to the body in some martial arts practices. These practices draw very heavily on the creative, emotional brain. Their teachers urge, "Get the feel for it. Get the feel for this technique."

We are also drawing on our body. How does the body move? What nerves are being stimulated? What muscles contract in a certain way for something to happen? How does my breath relate to the view through the scope? How does my body relate to the gravity anchoring me to the earth? The body is possibly the largest part of this process. None of it happens without the body.

At some point, the experiences begin integrating and becoming undifferentiated—we aren't thinking. The different systems begin to blend like the metals in the Japanese sword, and we are just doing. This is flow. It takes practice to allow the splits between the monkeys and elephant to fall away into one whole experience, but we get it a lot faster than we think. Once we get it, we never forget it.

Think about any skill and you'll see this process, even in a simple skill, like throwing darts. If you're throwing right-handed, you put your right foot forward and you grab the dart in a balanced way. All you do is throw it at a bull's eye. The skill requires a bit of eye-hand coordination, but that's an internal process blended with the external. You don't need big muscles. Anybody can do this. Anybody can learn how to throw darts in less than ten minutes. Getting that dart to the bull's eye is mental. If you have the process, you have what you need.

Whether we're long-range shooting, crafting a story, doing the dishes, or returning an email, we can do these as meditation-in-action. We all know how to wash dishes, but how do we do it without the monkeys and elephant split? That's the challenge. When we can do this, we can wash the dishes creatively, embodied, and maybe even storied. Washing the dishes becomes beautiful. Most importantly, we can do this typically boring task completely without resistance.

Unfortunately, our brains are not always in sync; they often fight each other. Our logical brain and our feeling brain tell our body to get to the gym and work out. The feeling brain feels in the mood. The left-brain knows it's the healthy thing to do. The body seems heavy and full of resistance; it's saying, "No, I don't want to." The monkeys love to fight and squabble. Half the monkeys may be trying to beat the elephant into behaving; a few may be rationalizing that you may be coming down with a cold, and it's best you stay at home. Yet another may be saying you can do it tomorrow. The elephant maintains, "I don't want to."

When we're in the present, the monkeys are quiet because there is no need for their opinion, no need for their constant chattering. The body and brain are integrated into a single, greater mind. This is your goal: To be able to integrate your brain and body into one mind so they are controlled by the greater you.

The process of getting the brain and body integrated and keeping them that way throughout the day is the result of organization. How do we get this to happen?

THE POWER OF ORGANIZATION: TECHNIQUES, PRINCIPLES, AND RESULTS

One of the best ways to become integrated, to achieve flow, is through organization. We tend to think of organization as the rows of socks neatly paired in the drawer for quick and easy access. Organization is not a result; it is a process. Just as the stabilization process is challenging at first, so too is learning to observe our patterns and tendencies, and then learning to organize them in a way to find balance, efficiency, and flow. With time, these skills of organized presence become the norm, and resistance falls away into a continuously unfolding path of Mastery. What was once a new skill becomes second nature.

Regardless of the task, an underlying external structure supports the organizational process. This structure keeps balance between the inner world and outer world. Recall that when we see the outer world beyond our inner world, and align them, we are operating in the reality we need in order to prevent sabotage.

Structure includes techniques, principles, and results. Techniques are simply standard processes for completing common actions. The more thought out a technique is into an efficient sequence of steps, the more powerful it is. Your principles are your guiding heuristics that apply to the specific task you need to complete. They are your procedures.

Returning an email, a very common day-to-day activity for most, provides an ideal illustration of how meditation in action works, and shows the role of structure and its components in this process. Some people have absolutely no problem with email, but Driven D2/D4s often struggle with such routine, mundane tasks. Some of us get a lot of email, with many very important messages, but the sheer volume of email is intimidating and causes us to procrastinate. The monkeys chime in, "Oh, I'll do that one later. I don't want to think about that right now. Oh, man, I don't want to respond to this."

This is self-sabotage in the making. Either you just don't respond, which becomes a problem, or you respond curtly or carelessly. The real issue is that you are not in the present. Your logical brain knows the email should be done, but it reminds you that you owe Joe a call. That is a good reason to put off the email. Your emotional brain complains that you're tired and you'll be more refreshed first thing in the morning. Your body feels restless and would like to go for a run; you're fighting the resistance in the body. As you can see, your body and mind are the opposite of organized, the opposite of being in sync.

A simple email meditation empowers you to align the brain and body and get you organized internally, but we need an external procedure to follow to guide internal organization. Each Driven will have their own personal approach to organization, but an understanding of the process will help develop a structure that works for you.

One helpful technique, regardless of the task, is to take care of any administrative procedures before you begin. As part of your preparation, you need to be certain that you will not be distracted. Remember, the goal is to be in the present as you respond to emails. That means no phone and no other windows or tabs open on your computer. People kill hours going back and forth between their email and their social media or scrolling through Facebook, which pulls them out of the present and keeps the internal disorganized. You are supposed to simply be answering email.

You might want to have a glass of water on your desk. If you get thirsty, you don't want to have to get up from the computer and be pulled out of your meditation. Randy sets aside time twice a day for email. He sets the mood with some music. Perhaps you don't want music, but a window opened for some fresh air. Regardless of your preferences, they should function to ensure you are not pulled out of the present for a real reason. The important takeaway is that you set the environment for success.

The final element of preparation is to introduce the needed level of stress. Driven D2/D4s need stress; they thrive and may even be addicted to it. However, too much stress pushes us toward the ends of our bandwidth where we start turning ropes into snakes. The key is identifying the right amount.

Good stress, known as *eustress*, creates a healthy tension, raises the heart rate, and increases focus. The ideal way to introduce eustress is through the stability practice of just focusing on one task while assigning a realistic time constraint. A time-driven goal introduces healthy stress, but also prevents the type of judgment inherent to setting quantity goals, whether dishes or email. The timer on your phone is perfect for this. It truly becomes a meditation practice with a starting bell and, twenty minutes later, an ending bell. This is not a race to see how much you can accomplish in the allotted time. Rather, it is a practice of focus and presence to just do this one task. Your mind and attention will wander. Gently return to the task over and over.

Our techniques establish the conditions for success. Our heuristics provide a framework or set of guidelines and procedures that increase efficiency, reduce expended energy, and eliminate burnout. Without this framework, we often use too much energy for our day-to-day tasks, which literally reduces our capacity to use our cognitive abilities to their fullest. If you set heuristics, you free up that cognitive energy from carrying your whole day around in your head and, unsurprisingly, you get a lot more done.

Think about how you answer emails. If you have a heuristic to guide your approach, you're not going to waste energy on unimportant emails, get frustrated, and self-sabotage by walking away from the computer. Your heuristic might tell you that if you come across an ambiguous email, you'll read the email and ask yourself, "What's the major concern? How do I address that concern; and, if I can't, who do I delegate it to? Is the energy in the elephant appropriate for the task at hand?" The Driven pause to take a few breaths and then return to the ambiguity with open curiosity. This is the meditative process.

When the timer goes off, you'll read through all those emails that you put into the draft folder. If you're happy with them, you'll go ahead and send. If you're not happy with them, you'll make a quick change and then send.

These heuristics are particularly helpful for tasks that include outliers, or situations that deviate from the expected. Most Driven people have the most difficulty figuring out how to address outliers, ambiguous events without a protocol. Having these guidelines empowers them to address these tasks. Additionally, without a real plan, tasks end up floating in our minds, which then amps stress into unhealthy levels and introduces sabotage when we forget to do them.

We need to assess our tasks for their actual importance in the real world. This assessment ensures that the elephant experiences a level of stress appropriate to the task. For emails, these principles include specific guidelines for what to do with ordinary, ambiguous, and urgent mail.

Doug categorizes tasks into have-tos (those with an impending due date), need-tos (those with a due date that is not immediate but will eventually turn into have-tos), want-tos (tasks without a due date that do matter but can be put off), and somedays (good ideas or wishes to keep note of). Having these in place ensures we aren't pulled out of the present by a situation we have not planned for. These heuristics help ensure that what's important in the real world fuels our drive.

As Driven, we tend to be distrustful, and we tend toward seeing hot stoves and snakes rather than reality; a rude email may ping our elephant. We must apply a reality check as we move ahead with the task, assessing the difference between a snake and a rope, and between the inner and outer world. If we think we see a rude email, we don't want to fly off the handle, interpreting the email incorrectly; we want to fully understand the sender's intent. If we act on impulse, believing the emotionally impulsive elephant and send a blasting email back, unwanted consequences can occur.

If you come upon a rude email—an email seemingly disrespectful—you just notice the elephant's radar pings, experience the emotion, watch (not listen to) the monkeys chatter, and assess how close you are to the top of your bandwidth. Take a DM pause until you can look at it objectively. Then come back to the logical container to hold this experience at a distance. What is the person really saying? What problem is this email addressing? Your logical brain will engage and brainstorm approaches or solutions. What is strategic and the best way to respond? When we are objective, our logical brain performs optimally.

Judgment and impulsive emotions cloud the ability to see the outer world—the real world. This sabotages us. If our brains and whole body are not aligned and integrated, if our emotional brain takes over entirely, we may become angry, see the email as evidence of our flaws, or blame ourselves. If we weren't so weak, stupid, childish (you can fill in the blank), then we'd have a better job, and we wouldn't have to deal with this nasty person. We're back to confirming the Driven D2/D4 shame-based, self-attack, and "if only" thinking. We are back to someone *who* this person doesn't like. We have lost track of *what* we are doing in this moment.

When our brains and body are coordinated, we don't go down this road. As we become more stable and meet the world with the logical container, we don't get internally disorganized when the elephant gets emotionally pinged and steers us in the sabotaging direction. We check whether this pinging is anything to worry about. With this integration of monkeys and the elephant, we are much less likely to have misunderstandings. We are objective.

We feel the ping in the elephant. We feel the emotion. We pause. We notice the impulse in the elephant to stomp on the email sender's head. However, we don't go on auto-pilot and just react. When the brain and body are in sync, the possibility of a nasty tone doesn't matter because right now, in the present, we just want to answer it.

With an organized approach to email or any activity in life, you approach a ping to the elephant with curiosity, enabling you to brainstorm and craft two to three concepts you want to incorporate. If you can't answer the email, file it to be forwarded to the person who can. If the email is important, put it in a draft folder and review it at the end of your allocated time, then send it. If you determine it's not strategic or in your best interests, you may choose not to answer it. Regardless of the specific approaches you draw on, you are drawing on your logical, planned techniques and principles. Whichever way you proceed, you are not sabotaged by the impulse.

You now see the role of techniques and principles. The final dimension is results.

Remember, Driven are wired to experience the world as

one in which everything can be done better. This is always true. That said, it is important to remember that emotionally charged sentiments like, "It wasn't good enough" is a habit we must break, because it leads to sabotage.

When we examine our results, remember that assessment is quite different from emotional judgment; it's a slippery slope from assessment to judgment if we aren't careful.

When the timer goes off, you assess your progress, but you must never believe the negatively charged emotional opinions about your performance. It is easy to slip into emotionally charged judgment if we set a goal of responding to twenty or thirty emails and end up having done just two. Then we're back to beating ourselves up and inviting self-sabotage.

Instead, observe your results with an objective, critical curiosity. Wonder why you only got two done this time. Look over the two emails. You may learn that these are significant emails. They might be life-changing emails, making the time you spent on them well worth it. You may have been performing this task right before lunch when you were hungry, and your monkey mind was bouncing all over the place. If we're curious as to how the process can be improved, we don't beat ourselves up; we don't judge ourselves. We know we've done okay with the emails, considering the real-life circumstances, and we know we can always do better. We learn to appreciate this feeling of being good enough but always accountable to how the process can be improved.

The ability to feel good emotions expands our bandwidth, motivating us to do what is good for us. We feel more equal to a task the next time, and less resistance to starting it. We remember the good experience. You understand you're creating, producing, conquering, or completing important things in your life (we will explore this further in Chapter 9, "Manifestation").

When you connect good emotions to the bigger concept of your purpose, that good feeling becomes more akin to excitement rather than fear. When we achieve, we begin to feel pride. Pride is a concept of accomplishment, intertwined with the concept of respect. Respect is experienced as having done the harder thing. We respect achievements that are not easy for most. Self-respect is the core of pride, not fear and not judgment that you are better than others.

While modern society presents pride as something positive, it can easily be confused with falsely inflated ego. When we associate accomplishment and achievement with positive fulfillment and purpose, we become motivated to continue that part of our life. We can then use these positive emotions to produce better results. Most importantly, these good emotions can fill our bodies in the present, replacing any resistance. If, however, we focus on the future accomplishments, then we are pulling ourselves out of the present and being pushed by fear of not becoming what we want. Randy describes the difference between having an ambition, which is wonderful, to being held by that ambition, which is sabotage.

Accomplishments that hold a valued social status can develop in us a *false sense of pride* or inflated ego. Navy SEALs, for example, influenced by the perceptions of others, idolize the idea of becoming a SEAL from the perspective of achievement. The same is true for obtaining a PhD. This false pride is wildly sabotaging. It is fear-based, grounded in the mindset that we *are* the accomplishments. We believe that the accomplishment will hide or at least distract others from our flaws—essentially the basis of the imposter syndrome.

When we focus on the perception of our accomplishments as a definition of our identity, we risk thinking of ourselves in terms of *who* rather than *what*. We become the guy *who* became a SEAL or the woman *who* earned her PhD. Our accomplishment becomes evidence of our worth. If we happen not to achieve the accomplishment, we see ourselves as failures who didn't cross the proverbial finish line. We are back to the cycle of self-sabotage.

By focusing on the effort and the enjoyment of the task rather than the shiny prize we think will transform us or prove our value, we enjoy a much richer life experience. We are free to examine those efforts to improve them, rather than aspiring toward a label we think will fix us.

It is remarkable how much simpler the world becomes with an organized internal balance. Structure offers us external support when the body and brain become disorganized, restricting our ability to self-sabotage through impulsivity or surrender.

See each task that's before you as part of your meditation practice. Set a timer for ten, twenty, or thirty minutes—something manageable and finite—so that you are time-driven and won't later be evaluating your success against a specific number of items completed. With time and practice, you're going to lose yourself in the process and you're going to be completely focused on the task. The efficiency that results from this practice is awe-inspiring. The goal is for you to completely become *what* you are doing, rather than thinking of yourself as a *who*—which can lead to thinking of yourself as someone *who* is slow, stupid, or whatever adjective you decide to shame yourself with because you didn't meet your goal. When the timer goes off, you've finished the activity, and because you met you time-restricted goal, you will have succeeded.

The internal organizational process takes time. Just like Japanese swords blending metals and becoming one, the mind and body take time and practice to work fluidly together. Being stable enough to know you are disorganized is key, and your subtle awareness will improve over time. Some situations will come easily; others may be a lifetime struggle. Start with the high-value activities, remembering to make maintainable small changes. Once you can experience the internal organization in a few simple activities and you've maintained the practice, you can expand the practice to optimize other areas of your life.

GETTING ORGANIZED

David Allen, author of *Getting Things Done*, or *GTD*, has built an organizational system that is simple, streamlined, and very effective—one that Driven D2/D4s can customize or borrow when developing their own systems. Allen's system is based on an organizational strategy often used around the house—he identifies containers that function as organizational tools.

The physical version of this type of system includes

containers or buckets designated for specific household objects. There is a bucket for books, a bucket for toys, a bucket for clothes. Allen applies this system to units of time as a way to organize our tasks into buckets based on due dates and priorities.

Each bucket is associated with a day. There is a bucket for today, for a week from today, for a month from today. Into the different buckets you toss the tasks. There is also a catch-all, inbox bucket into which can be tossed anything that hasn't already been placed into another bucket. Every day, you go through that inbox and examine the tasks. If you can do the task in two minutes, you do it right then. If not, you move it into the bucket for tomorrow or the next day or sometime before it is due. With this method, you can actually go through an inbox really, really quickly.

Most Driven D2/D4s appreciate the buckets; these buckets ensure that everything has a place and that there is a place for everything. However, many D2/D4s do not like routine or organization. This may be you. Regardless of your feelings towards organization, we do need these systems, because we are so creative, and because we think outside the box—as a result, everything is outside the box and this can get overwhelming.

A system of external organization allows us to more

productively go through the requirements of our lives. This is absolutely powerful for a Driven often overwhelmed by too many tasks and their associated due dates. Because Driven D2/D4s are multi-thinkers, constantly generating ideas, they may feel like they are in the midst of chaos. As a result, the more driven we are, the more obsessive-compulsive we get because we're dealing with a greater number of ideas and projects. A sound organizational system opens a space for creativity and supports your multi-thinking by preventing you from getting overwhelmed. When you finish clearing out the inboxes (a process that will now go much quicker with the DM practice) and get that time for creative thinking, designing, and building, you celebrate this success.

Organizational systems are a big part of the Military Planning Process. The military, in general, has an overarching strategy in any kind of warfare. That strategy may have multiple objectives, which each have tactics and missions to accomplish those objectives, all to achieve the desired outcome. The Military Planning Process factors in the reality that no plan survives the first contact with the enemy or the environment because there are so many variables that can't be anticipated; the environment will continuously change. To account for open-ended variables, the up-front planning is rigorous. Why do we plan if we know that nothing is going to go according to plan?

It develops a knowledge base and addresses as many variables as possible so that when we do get into the mix of conflict, we are not overwhelmed with a very large number of variables (both expected and unexpected); we can cognitively focus on just a few items.

The Military Planning Process identifies the most likely contingencies, unanticipated possibilities, and builds a contingency for as many of them as we have time for. We determine what is most likely to happen, and we know what to do should it happen—we are prepared. If somebody breaks a leg going to an objective, we know there's a rally point half-a-mile back. Everyone, including the helicopters, knows the location, because we already planned that helicopter-landing route. We know that if such a situation occurs, we must stop the operation and carry this poor guy the half-mile back. We've built that plan. Having a plan and a contingency plan (or plans) lets us get into the flow of life's operations. We take care of administrative issues first, just as we did in our email example earlier, and that allows us to get into the flow of just being in life.

When we have an external system to organize our thoughts and emotions—a system for putting our paint on canvas—and an internal structure to reduce our resistance, we begin to look at the world differently. This doesn't mean we view the world in utilitarian terms.

When we solely look at things in terms of their practical use, when we see things and focus solely on what they're good for, we're more likely to invoke our judgment.

Martin Heidegger reminds us that humans typically view the world in terms of what is useful; we look at a plant and think whether we can eat this or how it might look in our kitchen. We look at someone and think how this person can advance our career. While this is inarguably helpful for getting through life, it also serves to distort reality. That quick judgment prohibits us from seeing things within the context of reality; it becomes a screen or blinder. We miss the emotional reactions of our world and the depth of the moment-to-moment experience. We risk creating a separation between the inner and outer world.

A weed in the grass, for example, need not have a utilitarian function for us to appreciate it, though it may. Dandelions, just weeds, are edible, high in vitamin C, and useful to us. You can make dandelion wine and dandelion salad. You can make a root into a coffee. It's okay to see this usefulness, but what we have to recognize is that seeing the world only in terms of usefulness is seeing with our eyes only half-open. We want to see the world as it really is. Through meditation, through the practice of getting into reality and getting into the present, we can. From this practice, we can also look at the beauty in life.

THE SIX "F" WORDS

Humans see the world in terms of what Dr. Fernando Flores, a modern-day philosopher, calls permanent domains of human concern; aspects of life we must take care of to live a good life. According to Flores, there are thirteen of these domains. They are body, play, family, sociability, work, education, career, money, membership, world, dignity, situation, and spirituality. Using David Allen's bucket principle, we can ensure that these components stay organized. For purposes of a Driven's objectives, we can consolidate these domains into six simple buckets, each beginning with the sixth letter of the alphabet—the "F." These buckets are labeled: Friends, family, fitness, finance, fun, and faith.

We need to be able to keep all these balls in the air. We aren't balancing them, but rather keeping them in harmony. Balance suggests that we divide our time and effort equally across these buckets; this isn't the goal. Rather, we want to ensure that all these areas of our life are aligned so that our lives run beautifully. Think of an orchestra. At certain times, the violins will be carrying the music; at other times, it will be the horns or the percussion, but all of the instruments have a function and will play at some point. All are important to the piece. The parts the instruments play are not equivalent in duration and not all the instruments play every part of the piece, but each instrument contributes something vital.

Our life buckets are no different. If you dedicate yourself completely to your finances, what happens to your family or friends? What is your life like without those components? Driven are notorious for hyperfocusing on one area until one of the other areas can't be ignored any longer. This is sabotaging the inner organization and balance of our lives.

Our challenge is to get our logical brain's analytical and organizational skills, our feeling brain's creativity and emotion, and our body brain's intuition and guts into a flow for each of those life domains. The most critical factor is being in the present for each of the domains, for each of those buckets, and for each of your six F's. Even if you're planning for the future, you can still be present in what you're doing so that you are in a state of flow.

The body's emotional reaction holds the key to our insight into assessing each of these domains; but, our internal emotional stability must be in check, ensuring an accurate and realistic assessment when we shine a light on one of these areas. If we are feeling too stressed or overly positive, if we are too far from the center of our bandwidth, we can get an incorrect read on what area needs more attention.

We suggest you explore the F-buckets after a morning meditation in a systematic way. After ten or twenty minutes of DM, your stable CNS can give you a clearer picture of your whole life.

Following your morning DM, incorporate a tactic to ensure that your F-buckets are in harmony. You're not likely to find perfect balance. Doug always reminds his clients that he finds perfect balance about ten seconds a year, and these seconds are not in a row. Perfect balance is not the point. What we do want is a constant shift and adjustment of focus on the F's, depending on the different seasons of our week, month, year, and life.

If your wife and kids are off for spring break, your family may need more attention, and finances may need less. Other weeks, after a long grind at work, fun is definitely lacking in your life and that is where your focus needs to be. You need to consider and devote attention to all your F's, some to a greater degree than others depending on your circumstances.

Use of a journal or productivity planner is a great tactic when examining F-buckets. Use your journal to reflect on what you need to do to bring more harmony to your life. The journal or planner will guide you in addressing the six F's so that you keep life functioning the way you want it to.

We begin with a vision of your ideal harmonized life. Most

of us have trouble visualizing this ideal. What does it look like? Across Driven D2/D4s, our lives will look different. Remember, we want no guru; someone else's prescription for your life will not work. Become the artist of your own life. The harmony of the different buckets and an ongoing accurate assessment of that harmony will help reduce sabotage.

Begin by examining each bucket. What does your friends-bucket look like? Friends are a needed ingredient for all humans to have a sense of balance. We are a herding animal. Having friends is natural for us. Additionally, we live in a biased perception of reality. Friends can see the other side of the cup for us, and tell us about the handle we don't see. Friends offer opinions that support us; they are invaluable, but to develop that trust takes a time investment. Neglected friends are no longer friends.

How do I take care of these friends? When was the last time I contacted them? We all have acquaintances and business networks that we may call frequently. They too may be friends. Am I taking care of them? Can I get accurate feedback about other F-buckets in my life from them?

What about my family-bucket? What does it look like to take care of my family? How do I best take care of my parents, my children, my cousins, my in-laws? How can I best serve them that is within the context of my religious views, within my societal views, etc.? Are they a priority in my life? Casting judgment and guilt on one's self is not the point here; the goal is to consider making small changes to improve that area of your life.

How about fitness? Research has supported exercise as one of the most beneficial physical, emotional, and spiritual practices one can maintain. Generally, these benefits start at twenty minutes of moderate exercise three times per week. Some of us may completely neglect our bodies. The body is something that must be paid attention to or, eventually, it will force you to. However, there's a declining benefit from excessive amounts of fitness; we can easily overdo it or even become addicted to it. Driven D2/D4s tend to go to extremes, either ignoring exercise or becoming obsessive about it. Doug was an Ironman Triathlete and was clearly overdoing it. The other F's are hard to keep in balance when you are on a bike, swimming, or running thirty hours or more per week.

What does this fitness-bucket look like for you? Is the investment of time and energy appropriate? This obviously includes your diet as well. Sugar can be the Driven D2/D4s nemesis. Sugar is one of the most addictive known substances. Sugar enters our system and is similar to cocaine in its effect on our brains. It destabilizes our CNS. The little pop of dopamine that it releases can be too appealing to D2/D4's dopamine-starved elephant. Some people find eliminating sugar entirely to be helpful, but this can be quite hard for us. Sugar can be hidden, and quite often overlooked is the tremendous amount of sugar contained in alcohol. Cravings for a drink can be a hidden craving for sugar.

For finances, what is your ultimate vision, within reality, for how you want to be set up? Too many successful Driven D2/D4 entrepreneurs and professional athletes raise their standard of living as their income increases. We (Doug and Randy) guide our clients to settle into a comfortable standard of living that does not change based on business success.

One big payday should not change your standard of living dramatically. It is incredibly easy to sabotage with money. Remember, our genetics and brain structure are designed to live in a scary world. We are naturally prone to spend our savings down to the point that we must go out and make more. We are hunters designed to live in a world without refrigerators. We kill it. Eat it. Get hungry. Go kill another one. When we're financially secure, we lose our hunger, so we spend until we're hungry again. Farmers have grain silos to save for the winter. We're not wired like farmers, but nothing is better than a good CFP to hide our money from us to create this hunger artificially.

What about your fun-bucket? As discussed earlier, we may be prone to hide our need for dopamine from the world. We may feel that we don't deserve to go have fun if we are still trapped in the shame of not being good enough. Not getting our dopamine on a regular basis is sabotage. We eventually will start to crave it and create it in an impulsive way. Having it scheduled is key to avoiding sabotage. If you have an adventure to look forward to, even a small one, you will better tolerate the Wednesday afternoon work grind.

Tell your family about your dopamine need. Some of us are famous for hiding our need for dopamine, not telling our spouse about our weekend plans until the last minute, thinking it's easier to beg for forgiveness than ask for permission. This introduces guilt into our planned fun. Most of us find that coming home from a dopamine-filled vacation helps balance the other F-buckets. We are better spouses, family members, friends, and have better focus at work when we honor this fun-bucket. Getting our dopamine is not a choice; we need it. That said, this F can easily get out of balance. We don't get enough or we get too much. We need to consider the other F-buckets at the same time.

What about faith? This is possibly the most important F-bucket. Faith is not associated with a particular religion. Rather, it is a physical state in which we accept the logical, undeniable truth that the present moment is safe. We also accept that everything in the world is exactly as it should be. That is the element of faith. We don't believe that it can't get better; it can always be better. But it is safe; it is okay. If you choose to add to this understanding—the religious orientation—that there is an order to everything, all the better.

The physical experience of faith is key to stabilizing the CNS. A spiritual experience of an inner peace beyond understanding can change how you see the world and how quickly you make progress in stabilizing and organizing your inner and outer worlds. Having further belief that things will work out in an orderly way in the future can help the monkey mind calm down quickly. Either way, having a preplanned, methodological practice to experience the present moment as safe is critical to life change, and will increase your efficiency in every task.

When we look at all our F-buckets as a collective whole, we have to reflect on what is best for us using that curiosity which is so powerful. We must continuously ask, "*What am I?*" I am Driven. My genetics are different. Why am I doing what I'm doing? Where is this leading me? We want to be purposeful in what we do. When we align our monkey mind, body, and our heartfelt purpose with a task, we are manifesting and clearly experiencing our purpose.

BEING TRUE TO YOURSELF

All people live in a semi-tuned-out state, with their past experiences biasing the expectations they have of the future. Driven D2/D4s may be more tuned out than most. When we are hyperfocused on the next shiny thing on the horizon, we are tuning out things we probably should not; we may be neglecting any one or more of our F-buckets. Our intense, almost obsessive focus is one of our greatest gifts, but it's also one of our greatest risks for sabotage. Once you have learned to stabilize and then build a strong logical container to organize your landscape, putting external structures in place to help maintain internal organization, you are ready to look deeply into your life.

Most Driven D2/D4s are filled with a lot of resistance to this self-examination. We especially do not want to overly manage our thoughts and impulses; we don't want to try to be a perfect citizen in a safe world. We are scared that this organization, this structure that allows us to "get control of our crazy selves," will prevent us from having fun (getting our dopamine). We worry about losing the spark that drives our greatest successes, and we don't want to be trapped by the expectations of the farmer's world.

We are different and should live different lives from those wired without our gifts. We just want to be the ones making the choices. We want to make decisions with our brain integrated and aligned, choosing our path, and not having our direction chosen for us. Stabilization and organization provide the harness we need to control that drive so we determine where it leads us.

As Driven, we can ride the wild horse and risk being thrown off, or we can tame that steed so that it will take us where we want to go. If we give into our impulsive instincts, to addiction, to pleasure-seeking, we become a slave to these habits. Eventually, somebody else will take charge of our life, be it a spouse, therapist, judge, or police officer. We might even wind up in prison. (That's why many D2/D4s join the military. This allows them to give control over to a trusted agent so that they can eventually learn how to take control of themselves.)

Our creativity, compulsive energy, wealth of ideas, and passion may be overwhelming and we want to have some control in our lives. For some Driven D2/D4s, this need for control manifests in obsessive-compulsive tendencies or even Obsessive-Compulsive Disorder (OCD). The OCD is our way of creating structure. Unfortunately, when the OCD is profound, we can develop anxiety and uncontrolled, impulsive self-sabotaging behavior if we're forced to change our plans.

If those with OCD look at these tendencies as a gift, and develop a curiosity about those events that don't go according to plan, they start to embrace their landscape from a place in their hearts rather than reacting to it from fear. This fear creates a deep shame and results in our believing we don't deserve to relax and have fun. This can create tremendous resistance to all that is possible in our lives; we believe we don't deserve what is good.

We find freedom from our fear when we have a greater purpose for our lives. This becomes possible if we catch those pings in our elephant and manage the impulses associated with them. If we only make small changes that can be kept and integrated into our routines, we will succeed.

The Mastery Path is never pushing too hard in any one area, but also never giving up the pursuit of being better in every area of our lives. It is feeling safe and content in the moment but never being satisfied with what we are becoming. Driven D2/D4s are made for this state of continuously improving our lives. Once the practice of finding greater internal CNS stability and an externally stable path is your norm, you are ready to begin to manifest a full and successful life.

· CHAPTER 9 ·

MANIFESTING YOUR FUTURE

"No work or love will flourish out of guilt, fear, or hollowness of heart, just as no valid plans for the future can be made by those who have no capacity for living now."

—ALAN WATTS

Meditation practitioners use a riddle to deepen their understanding of being in the present. One such riddle is, "When you finally reach the top of a one-hundred-foot pole, what is the next step?" Your logical linear monkeys, if asked this question, may answer that there is obviously something to do after you finally reach your goal.

"Climb down? Jump?" If the emotional monkeys start to chime in, they probably ask, "Relax? Take a breath? Pick another pole?"

The teacher will simply reply, "Wrong answer, more meditation!" to these responses. Eventually, the frustration at being repeatedly wrong gets the impulsive goal-driven elephant involved and makes even engaging the question more and more difficult emotionally. "How will it feel when I eventually get it right? Am I too stupid to get the right answer?" Frustration and self-judgment persist until the split between the monkeys and elephant eventually disappears.

The question itself has become another pole to climb. We keep trying for the answer, seeking the perfect response, just as we seek this perfection in other areas of our lives—looking for that ideal job, spouse, house, child, or achievement. With meditation, you recognize the parallel this question has to your own life and you finally look for the answer in the present moment.

The meditative practice of answering these types of questions is to completely "eat" the question until it is fully and unconditionally understood in every part of your being. Eventually, the answer comes to you; almost as if you have been struck by lightning. You may find yourself laughing, thinking once again, there you are, doing what you may have done all your life—looking for the finish line, believing that getting the right answer will make you feel good about yourself at last.

You may have been struggling for years with a question for which the answer is obvious, and has been the whole time. When you finally see the answer, the split between the mind and body is gone; the observer falls away, and a deep spiritual truth becomes known. Often, we laugh at ourselves. We never forget this experience.

There is only one answer to the riddle about what to do when you reach the top of that one-hundred-foot pole. That answer is, "There is no pole."

We're constantly creating worlds in which there exists an illusion that if we can jump over a hurdle, earn a certain amount of money, have a particular title, or climb a one-hundred-foot pole, we will at last feel rewarded or safe. The key word in this statement is illusion. There is no pole. There never was a pole. These poles, these achievements, exist because of the emotional and mental discontentment and fear that we aren't good enough now, but with a particular accomplishment, maybe we will be okay. This belief is a horrible trick of the mind and essentially a part of the human condition.

For the Driven D2/D4, this discontented condition may be intolerable. The constant striving, constant craving, and constant driving toward the future is propelled by the belief and emotion that we're not good enough now. When you finally get that you're okay now, but you can always be better—when you truly understand that better has no finish line—you will experience fully that there is no pole.

DROPPING THE FEAR THAT DRIVES YOU

Many Driven D2/D4s find that one of the significant obstacles to creating a new world is that they are afraid to give up the fear that drives them; they believe fear is their fuel. They worry that without this fear, they won't work hard anymore. Working hard is what they know and it has created a lot of wealth for them.

Driven D2/D4s need to recognize that fear and drive are not the same. We are Driven and will always have drive as our core essence, but it need not be grounded in fear. When we internalize the difference between fear and drive, we don't slow down—we just become more efficient and directed.

When you understand that it is normal for you, as a Driven, to be very sensitive to danger and to fear, that it is normal for you to need opportunities to get your dopamine; that any unrewarded feelings are normal and not indicative of a problem, and when you understand that you are okay in the present, you can stabilize. You can organize the F-buckets of your life so that they support your needs and empower you to reality-check your fear. You can look to the future as an opportunity to become better—as something that goes on forever, rather as a single point on a psychological map, because better has no finish line. As Driven D2/D4s, we have the drive to attain our objectives, but we need to be focused enough to know what those objectives are. We need to have our brain integrated into a grounded, stable body so that we make the most of our unique abilities. But then, what drives us? If we lose our fear, what is our fuel?

EMBODIED EMOTIONAL INTENTION

Imagine you are a salesperson with an important presentation to make. As a Driven, you want to caution against thinking about this presentation from a place of fear, from thinking of it as another pole to climb. You don't want your fear or a fixed ideal to drive your sales presentation. You don't want to think in terms of 100, 90 or even 50 percent of the audience buying your product; nor do you want some dollar amount in sales as a goal, as proof of your sales ability. This outcome-based focus creates a false sense of pride. It's also the route to sabotage.

As discussed earlier, pole climbing is a "lose-lose" endeavor. If you don't achieve your goal, you have proof of your inadequacies, proof that you're a broken salesperson. A less obvious but more serious consequence is the customers may sense your fear-based intention. When customers sense that you must make the sale at any cost, they will feel that your intention is selfish and not in their best interest. No matter how charming you are, they will be turned off.

You don't want a measurable goal, a point on the map to prove your excellence, a goal you can miss, a goal that emanates self-interest. Such a goal makes the whole process about you rather than your customer. Such a goal takes you from thinking about the experience of selling in the present to a future, ego-fueling goal. Rather than focusing on how much you sell, envision instead entering the room excited because you believe that you can help the people by sharing information about your product. This altruistic emotional excitement fills your body, and your mind becomes free and curious, with no fear-based expectation of how the desire to help your customer will be met.

Enthusiasm is infectious. Your customers are going to feel your excitement. You have no hidden agendas. Your sincere desire for good intentions shines through so your customers are receptive.

For you, it's not about making a sale, but about creating a world where you are helping people who, in return, will compensate you with money or business. This may seem like a subtle distinction, but it's huge. It's a shift from a mindset where the goal is a sale that may or may not happen, to one where the goal *has already happened* before you walk into the room, and then continues to unfold and direct your behavior in a moment-to-moment experience. The goal and process become one and the same.

A deeply felt, other-directed, positive emotional intention—a desire to help others becomes the driver of your behavior. Instead of being driven by a fear of not doing well and confirming your perceived inadequacies, you're carrying an embodied sense that you are there to help make another person's life better. Regardless if the person buys your product, you have succeeded. If they do make a purchase, the product or service will enrich their lives in some way. If they don't, they have held onto their money because the product wasn't a fit for their needs.

Once you let go of ego-fueled poles and instead embrace an emotional desire to make the world better, you won't need to automatically react to every ping of the elephant. With practice, you will be able to use the logical container to catch and reality-check the subconscious elephant's impulses and observe the chattering monkeys. You'll be able to expand your consciousness so you aren't working on autopilot; your brain and body will be connected. You will have a space to explore your emotional intentions before they turn into action.

When we apply this practice to each of the F-buckets, we can obtain clarity and freedom from fear. We can manifest a life congruent with how we desire to feel. If you are in a relationship, married, or have kids, the family-bucket is a nice place to start emotionally manifesting a change in your life. You will almost immediately feel the result of freedom from guilt and fear. Rather than thinking, "*Who* am I?" as a partner or parent, you think, "*What* am I?" doing right now.

When we spend time with our partner or kids, we embody the emotional intention of love, care, support, strength, compassion, and the desire to fully listen to them. We can feel this emotional intention in our body. We replace self-doubt, fear, worry, guardedness, and defensiveness with a calm clarity that we are being our intention.

How we behave with our family becomes a natural expression of how we are feeling. We aren't focused on the outcome; we aren't focused on a pole to climb, but rather on the present intention. You're not watching yourself do something, evaluating yourself like a critic reviewing an actor. You're being your actions. Your predetermined moral beliefs and an elephant filled with emotion and energy carry out your beliefs. You become the Japanese sword of blended metals, integrating your moral intention with the embodied emotion. This is manifestation.

Extending this embodied emotional manifestation to all the F-buckets is a lifelong process, one that dramatically changes your landscape. You consciously determine how to manage your buckets. This means you enjoy a guilt-free, dopamine-filled vacation because you have addressed the other F-buckets. You're comfortable with your finances because you don't have a fixed goal that you must meet as evidence of your success. You're empowered to maintain vital friendships because you have time for them. You are okay with your commitment to fitness because you don't react to the elephant or the monkeys. All these areas are also explored to fully meet your intention. All of them can be improved as they naturally change through the seasons of your life.

Manifesting your faith is possibly the most powerful F-bucket of them all. The feeling that we are on the right path is extremely liberating, especially for those of us who've felt fear and self-judgment most of our lives.

When the elephant does get pinged and a wave of negative

emotion fills your body, you don't have to be defensive. You no longer have to assume others are attacking you or questioning your intention. Your intentions are clear—you know what your side of the cup looks like and can meet the ping with calm curiosity.

Instead of automatically reacting, you ask with embodied, compassionate curiosity, "What are you doing? Why are you reacting the way you are?" You ask about their emotional intention in the moment, and question what is happening in their inner world. You are then able to look from their side of the cup for the handle you are not seeing and seek to understand their perceptions. When we are clear with our embodied emotional intention, we hold our ground without the need to pull away or push them away. We convey our intention, which includes a desire to understand and encourage others to examine their own inner world and its implications for their behavior.

When we have learned to understand our own embodied emotional intention, we can take this understanding one step further and lead with it, better connecting with others because we're better able to take their perspective. That is what curiosity allows us to do. Rather than letting a knee-jerk reaction direct our exchanges, we question others' perspectives of the cup, and we understand how powerful that perspective can be. The emotional intelligence we need in order to read others' intentions will dramatically improve. We immediately feel freedom from shame and fear.

You should not take this new power lightly. The change in you will be significant. Others may almost immediately sense that you are different. This is particularly true if you have led a shame-filled Driven life, and others are used to you being on guard and defensive; now, you are no longer reactive. This change can be dramatic and almost immediate, which can be unsettling for many people. It is likely you will be able to see others much more clearly, particularly their emotional reactions and defensiveness. We cannot encourage you strongly enough to learn quickly to be gentle with your observations and be sparse in your analysis. People not on the Mastery Path have a much more difficult time with personal accountability and your observations may be taken as criticism. Doug often says one of the greatest lessons the meditation cushion has taught him is to just shut up. Listen more and talk less.

EMOTIONAL AND LOGICAL VISUALIZATION

Humans want to feel the familiar. What is familiar is not frightening; the unfamiliar can be. Even what is normally highly stressful and scary is less scary if you have experienced it before. This phenomenon makes for a powerful tool for Driven D2/D4s.

Through visualization, you can emotionally experience the future. When you rehearse how something is going to be in the future, you get to feel what your body is going to feel when you are in that situation.

For Driven D2/D4s, this can be life-changing. Most of us have spent our lives scared of the future, using much of our mental power planning contingencies for possible worst-case scenarios. Few could argue that being prepared for the worst is without merit; we can all think of situations where this has saved us from disaster.

We are not suggesting you go blindly into the future hoping for the best. We are suggesting quite the opposite. You want to know the future but to know it on a physical level—to know it with your mind and body organized. An accurate view of the future helps us discern snakes from ropes and ropes from snakes. If you are stabilized and have created an organized routine, you have the ability to become very skilled at avoiding mistakes and identifying opportunities.

The practice is simple. You visualize yourself in a scenario where you're succeeding at a task, such as closing a big deal, having an investment pay off, or enjoying another business success. Picture the situation in as much detail as possible—the sights, the sounds, the smells, the people around you, the congratulatory phone calls you might receive after, and what might be posted on Facebook. See the reactions on your family's faces, hear the accolades from your friends, and imagine how this situation would change your life.

If your visualization is realistic, not everything will be positive. Some of your friends may be jealous. The increased financial security may create more problems than you anticipated. You need to ask yourself relevant questions. How would you handle it? How would it change your life? What unforeseen issues might arise? What would you feel? (This step can prepare you for issues you may not have thought of before.) Feel all that emotion in the body.

The next step is to question what greater purpose this success means for your life and the world. Is it just to alleviate your fear of financial insecurity? Is it false pride and ego hoping to impress your friends or family? How would it benefit your family? Does it align with your greater purpose? This questioning helps you to see what your greater purpose is. Rather than defining yourself as the one who succeeds, you want to shift your focus fully into what you are doing in the moment. What is the emotional intention driving this success?

The power of emotionally embodied rehearsal has been proven time and again. In the classic study of mentally practicing shooting baskets, those who mentally rehearsed shooting baskets got better faster than those who rehearsed by physically shooting the baskets. That makes sense when you think about it. It is nearly impossible to have ten perfect shots in a row when you're doing it in real time, in real life. When you rehearse, you've giving yourself a trial run at perfection.

By rehearsing, you're letting your elephant be present and comfortable with this familiar and less-intimidating experience. You're not creating a safe world, but rather a familiar world. When things happen, because they are familiar, you're ready for any contingencies and possibilities. The elephant is not going to be sending those distress impulses up to the other brains because it sees nothing dangerous. It is just business as usual.

When the body feels before you act, you have the enormous advantage of being familiar with the feelings of success. You expand your bandwidth to this possibility; you are comfortable with the feelings, and you avoid the sabotage that arises when you aren't comfortable.

If you start becoming familiar with the new world you're creating, even before you've created it, this new world will naturally evolve. Because you've rehearsed an experience, maybe ten times or maybe one-hundred times, when you walk into your situation, the experience will be second nature. If you feel you've already knocked it out of the park, the people around you are going to feel that too, and they will give you feedback physically. You then create a self-fulfilling prophecy of success.

Rehearsal has to involve the body. You might rehearse something in your head repeatedly, but that doesn't come close to feeling what it's like to really nail it. Without that physical feeling component, we're missing something important.

Consider the example of the salesperson we discussed earlier. If your primary purpose is to help others, it will be easy to walk into any room without fear of failure, because as we discussed, your goal is to help the people in your audience; whether they buy or not, you have achieved your goal.

Imagine yourself walking into the room embodied with the desire to help. First, you focus on the fact that you must teach people about your product so they can make an informed decision about a possible purchase. Your logical brain knows all your product's features. Your emotional brain is excited about the product. Your body is clear in its desire to help.

If you see yourself in that moment, meeting the audience around you, you can practice getting the brain and body aligned. If you start to feel like you're losing a customer, you don't let fear drive your actions; you don't let fear control the other brains. You fall deeper into your intention and intuitively pause. The fear you felt is replaced with a genuine desire for helping the people seated before you. Your curiosity reflects this objective. "Do these people want to be helped? Do they understand what my product can do for them? Is this the wrong product or service for them?" Driven D2/D4s are often good at connecting others. If you cannot help your customer, maybe you know someone who can.

You aren't afraid. You aren't judging. You are simply curious about the people before you, curious about how you can help them.

Fast-forward and you're there at the sales meeting. The feelings you have are familiar, as you have already felt those feelings during rehearsal. Because they are familiar, they are not frightening. Manifesting a future based on this general sense of emotional outcomes can help expand your bandwidth in a positive direction, so when your life begins to change for the better, you are less prone to sabotage.

Rehearsal is much more powerful if we draw on prior experiences to identify strengths, techniques, and strategies that went well previously. Remember what it felt like and feel it in the body now. As you do this, bring this positive emotion into the body as fully as possible. Then bring the new situation into mind and place these good feelings into the new context. You can also draw on what didn't seem to work in the past from a mindset of curiosity, not judgment, sifting through the strategies that were good or not so good, and feeling what it is like to use them.

Multi-thinking ability is a valuable asset in the visualizing and rehearsal process. As Driven D2/D4s, we can better anticipate the obstacles and the advantages that will present themselves. We can multi-think the multitude of things we need to experience or might experience in any situation. We can multi-think the potential questions our client or spouse might have. We can see things from a great many angles, and we can create intricate contingency plans.

This can become overwhelming, however, and needs to be done from a stable and organized place. Then we can establish the variables on a timeline and sort through issues, identifying the important ones. By rehearsal and visualization, we are making them more obvious. We are preparing the body and mind simultaneously. Envisioning yourself in a future moment can help you organize yourself internally, and it allows you to order the tasks to best accomplish your intention.

MANIFESTING YOUR PURPOSE

Manifesting is not creating an internal cheerleader. Manifesting is creating a realistic person who knows and is directed by their purpose, not by a fear of not being good enough. To make other people our focus, you have to be okay with you. In a sense, you must step out of the picture so only your task is before you. Once you start thinking about yourself, it's no longer about other people.

Regardless of the context, you want to be okay in the moment. You want to know there are no poles to climb.

Doug remembers creating one of these poles when he was getting his PhD. He had the clarity to know that his purpose was to teach others not to sabotage their lives as he had done early in his. (Doug dropped out of high school at seventeen and was basically couch surfing at his friends' houses, or living in a car.) Obviously, in the intervening ten years, he realigned his path and found his calling in helping others. Still, he struggled.

As a Driven, he decided early in his graduate work that a dual PhD in Industrial/ Organizational Psychology and Clinical Psychology might prove his worth. However, Doug saw himself as a *who*. In his inner world, he wasn't someone *who* had a PhD. As such, he felt a tremendous amount of resistance to starting the process. Yet, his deeper inner purpose pulled him forward nonetheless. The PhD was the shiny prize he idolized—the proof that he was an intelligent, successful person. For all his years at school, he saw the PhD as the finish line in the distance.

His journey was full of poles. One such pole was a huge number of resources he needed to read to get good enough to begin writing the dissertation. He read enormous amounts of material, but did no writing. He felt he wasn't ready. He hadn't yet reached the top of that pole.

While his deeper purpose never wavered, for eighteen months he read everything he could about his topic (which was, interestingly, self-sabotage and self-fulfilling prophecy) waiting to feel smart enough to start the dissertation. He did no writing. He didn't appreciate the irony of his reading about the very thing occurring in his life until his dissertation was completed.

Roughly 50 to 80 percent of the people who start dissertations do not finish. They're called ABDs—folks who have completed all but the dissertation. That possibility loomed before Doug.

Eventually, Doug was jolted out of his inner world, where he was not capable of earning the PhD. What helped him align his inner and outer world to become one world was the realization that plenty of people with PhDs around him were, in his eyes, complete idiots. He realized that if others could do it, so could he. He was good enough at that moment, and his purpose became embodied. He could be better, but he was good enough now. His resistance began to dissolve.

Resistance is just the product of our creating a pole that seems too tall to climb. Once we recognize there is no pole, our resistance dies away. However, even once we move past that initial resistance, we have to be on guard for other sabotaging mechanisms. If we still experience ourselves as inadequate in some way—if we still hold onto an internal reality of ourselves as not good enough—any progress we make will move us too close to the outer ends of our bandwidth, and the elephant's resistance will get stronger.

For Doug, typing his dissertation would move him close

to the top of his bandwidth, and suddenly, his elephant would start to take over. He termed this "light ass syndrome," because he'd feel like standing up and stepping away from the computer. (Over the next year, these breaks became very productive, since he dealt with the syndrome by looking for household jobs that just had to be done. Even the junk drawer was immaculate.)

Eventually, his obsession became his front lawn. He had his lawn and gardening equipment by the front door and would walk out and go work on the lawn. He had the most perfectly manicured lawn in the neighborhood, if not the city. In OCD fashion, every blade of grass was the same height; every sprinkler worked perfectly. From a distance, it was amazing, but on closer inspection, its odd perfection gave everyone the shivers.

Because he'd get up from the dissertation to go out to the front garden for twenty to thirty minutes and feel immediately rewarded by what he was doing, his body could stabilize. His embodied purpose would once again become clear, and he could get back to the computer. His inner world would calm down and he'd know he was okay. Then he could move ahead with what he needed to do. In a way, the lawn work kept him from writing, but it also facilitated it.

The guiding principle in manifestation is having a purpose

in your life that is bigger than you, and then incorporating the inner and outer organization principles to get it accomplished. If your focus is about you, it isn't about the present nor about a greater purpose. If your focus is about you, it's usually coming from a place of fear. It's about proving to yourself that you're not broken or flawed. With that mindset, you're going to go back to the riddle and continue to look for a pole that you have to climb to feel okay—only there's always going to be another pole, and you're never going to feel okay. When you shift your focus to the other person, you are shifting your thinking and your way of being away from fear.

Purpose is not a complex analysis of the existential reasons why you are on the planet. It is actually very simple. Any reason that is bigger than you is enough. Helping the world and making it a better place is good enough as long as you can embody the emotion and feel the intention.

Most people's thoughts are self-centered. Even when we think we're focusing on other people, we are usually wondering what they think of us; this means we're not actually thinking about them. We're still thinking about ourselves.

Self-focus is usually driven by fear—fear of failure, fear of not being good enough. If you're constantly judging and evaluating yourself, then you're watching yourself.

Thinking about others only happens when you can drop the concern about yourself.

Driven people tend to think of themselves; we're often narcissistic. We fixate on proving ourselves as wonderful, spectacular, flawless people. We judge ourselves, assembling proof of our flaws and our brokenness, collecting evidence of our failings, and then assembling a super-high pole that if we climb will invalidate all of our findings. This is narcissism at its core.

We say, "I need a big car. I need a beautiful wife. I need the big house. I need these things, because without them, others might see the deeper, darker flawed me and these things will disguise that."

Sometimes people put a poster on their wall of what they want their lives to look like. You probably know people who have a picture of a skinny model in a bikini on their refrigerator to keep them from eating, or a photo on their desk of a Porsche in front of a fancy house to keep them at their desk. Motivational gurus tell them if they believe in the picture, if they envision the bikini or the car, they will eventually obtain these achievements.

Nothing is further from the truth. These posters are nothing but poles. You look at the skinny model and you end up eating a bunch of junk food to deal with the feelings of being broken. These pictures keep you from manifesting, because you're once again back to the mindset that you are currently defective.

Just reading, "Today, I'm not going to smoke," doesn't change you internally. Manifesting has nothing to do with making a poster of what you want or reciting some words on a sheet of paper. Manifesting is actually experiencing in your body what it's like to already have what's in the poster.

The posters are unnecessary. The disguises are unnecessary. They are based upon a flawed premise that there's something wrong with you. There's nothing wrong with you. Through meditation, you finally recognize this. It's like zooming out on Google Maps. You get a bigger perspective of your entire life. You see where you've been. You also see where you're going. There is no judgment.

When we teach DM to shooters, and people hit the target at 1,000 yards multiple times, they experience something remarkable. They feel genuinely good in their whole body. All at once they feel safe. They feel present. It's almost overwhelming. People sometimes break into tears coming off the gun. They have done something that minutes before they doubted.

The stronger the Drive is in someone, the more unfamiliar that good feeling is. Some of us have never allowed ourselves to really feel it our entire lives. Most people want to get up and run away from that good feeling. We (Randy and Doug) tell them to just allow that good feeling to happen, to just be with it.

It is a life-changing experience for most people. They had no idea they could feel that good and safe at the same time. Their desire to hit the target and just experience the wonderment at being alive is the deeper purpose.

This is manifestation. You have done something the monkey mind could not comprehend on its own. You are finally allowing yourself to feel these good feelings and be present to those good feelings without jumping onto another pole as fast as you can. Rather than feeling the resistance to the future, you're riding the wave of the present, letting it gently push you forward. You're not fighting anything, especially not yourself.

Manifestation sets us on this Mastery Path. On this path, we can always be better. We always have something to work on. This is an ideal mindset for a Driven, because you naturally have that inclination (particularly if you are D4) to be looking to the horizon. That horizon is still there; no one's taking that away from you, but you are now comfortable that it goes on forever—that you will never get there, and that is fine—because right now, in the present, you are fine.

Manifesting doesn't change your drive; it just directs it. It empowers us to make decisions that are not driven by fear. Yes, fear may have been what you depended on to achieve, but fear prevents you from controlling your destiny.

When we meditate and get our inner and outer world aligned, we finally can answer, "Do I really want to make this future for myself?" This is dramatically different from the, "I don't want to, but I feel I have to" mindset that comes from fear-based thinking. Your decisions aren't the product of reflexive, defensive actions originating in a biased world, but rather decisions based on what you want in the real world.

· CHAPTER 10 ·

DRIVEN IN A SAFE WORLD

"The key is to keep company only with people who uplift you, whose presence calls forth your best."
—EPICTETUS

It is not easy to be different, nor for that matter is it easy to be around people who aren't different.

People see our Driven natures as self-destructive. They see our multi-thinking as tangential and even mind-boggling, our thrill-seeking as crazy, and our perfectionism as unreasonable. They find us condescending. They judge our Type A natures and say we have addictive personalities.

To the Driven, the rest of the world seems slow, stupid, and lazy. A plodding, color-within-the-lines approach to life frustrates us. We don't easily tolerate a willingness to accept good if great is possible. We may hurt others' feelings easily. The differences between Driven and non-Driven can create friction and conflict.

If you are Driven, you can attest to that friction. The old adage, "One man's meat is another man's poison," aptly describes the origin of this friction. For the Driven, the thrill of risk is our meat; in fact, without it, we will feel as if we're starving. For the safe world, risk-taking is plain poison. People who aren't Driven seldom get their minds around the motivation to take the kind of chances we are comfortable with.

Although the nature of the Driven may seem at odds with the safe world and many of the people in it, they can complement each other in ways that make for a very strong team. Once you are well along on the Mastery Path, you will develop the insight to recognize where these differences become a huge asset. Driven and those who are not wired this way each bring strengths to any relationship or task. By closely examining the differences, we're better able to see where the Driven and the non-driven can support each other in our professional and personal lives.

Understanding and accepting these variances without judgment is the first step to developing amicable relationships. Judgment is the greatest obstacle to developing harmony. You recall the story of the client who hated cups without handles—he grew angry because he perceived that someone was going to hand him a cup with no handle. The client judged the situation without a true picture of the situation for the person handing him the cup, and without knowledge of the real world. From his angle, the cup looked like it had no handle; in actuality, it did have one.

Seeing the world from another person's perspective will alleviate many of the conflicts between yourself and the non-Driven people in your life. Your curiosity and growing emotional intelligence will foster that perspective taking.

DRIVEN IN THE WORKPLACE

The differences between Driven and non-Driven individuals have enormous benefits in the workplace. Most organizations require the contributions of people all along the continuum of Driven D2/D4s and non-Driven to be successful.

Those without Driven attributes are an ideal fit for a variety of critical jobs that D2/D4s could not or would not want to do. In primordial times, the person tolerant of boredom was the basket weaver. These baskets held the meat, tools, pelts, and other artifacts necessary to society. The job of the basket weaver was highly important. Also of critical importance were the jobs of the hunter and guard, the jobs Driven took on. The Driven caught the animals to produce the meat. They protected the cave from the saber-toothed tiger.

Today, there is not much need for basket weavers, and Saber-tooth tigers are no longer an issue, but modern-day roles for both Driven and non-Driven still exist. Those without Driven wiring are genetically and biologically suited to be the company accountants, keeping the finances organized so the Driven can bring in sales or brainstorm new products. Both are necessary.

The unique characteristics of both Driven and non-Driven complement each other, making for very strong and vital relationships once we understand each other's needs and capitalize on each other's gifts. Most people like routine; Driven D2/D4s like surprises. Most like the security of slow growth and few risks. This type of security can be painfully boring for Driven. The workplace offers opportunities for a broad base of orientations and characteristics.

Many Driven D2/D4s are suited to get out there and sell;

we have the resilience to remain undaunted if we don't make the sale. We continue to persevere. Driven D2/D4s are willing (and eager) to take risks, so many fit well in a product development role. Usually a person's professional history provides insights into a person's degree of drive and where this person best fits into an organization.

Randy had upward of fifteen employees and about forty contractors in his first business. Coming from the SEAL Teams, he was used to working with Driven types. Randy was smart enough to hire non-Driven people to do things that Drivens didn't want to do, but he treated all his employees as if they were Driven, whether or not they actually were. He assumed they were all comfortable with the risk-taking and think-on-your-feet skills of Driven SEALs.

Driven and non-Driven understand the world differently, and in turn, respond accordingly. Randy didn't understand these differences and was not as gentle with his direction as he is today. (Although his coaching clients can attest he is still a SEAL at his core and will push them to the edge.) When he pushed hard, incentivized employees by giving them bonuses based on new ideas and new concepts or risk-taking, many looked at him with blank stares. This approach didn't work for the employees not wired like the Driven, though it did work for the few Driven D2/D4s he brought in.

As such, there are enormous benefits to placing people in jobs that fit their psychological profile. The Myers-Briggs instrument provides insights into fitting a person to a particular organization and role. (Interestingly, there is now research suggesting that many of the attributes assessed in the Myers-Briggs test are genetic, like introversion/extroversion and a feeling/thinking orientation.) In much the same way that we wouldn't place an introvert in a cold-call sales position, we wouldn't place a Driven in a clerical role. A Driven required to do rote work is not likely to perform well, if they even last.

That is not to say that the Driven or non-Driven traits are immutable. While genetics and brain structure may be the underlying determinate for drive, genetic predispositions can be altered; the science of epigenetics explains the variety of variables that impact the manifestation of drive.

Experience has an impact on drive. Suppose, for example, a child grows up in an impoverished, abusive household where lack of money creates an environment of fear and insecurity. His early home life is filled with chaos, fighting, and unhappiness directly connected to financial insta- bility. Essentially, this child has lived through a trauma. As a result, he may come to see money as all-important and become much more driven to obtain money and become wealthy than he might otherwise be. He is afraid of poverty; he has seen and experienced firsthand what it can do and never wants to experience that life again.

Is this person a Driven? If he meets the description then yes, he is, although he may not have all the biological markers. He has learned to live in a world full of fear and danger. Whether his experiences affected his genetics, these experiences have shaped his responses, reactions, and goals. Likewise, a genetically wired Driven who is beaten down by the world's judgment may no longer draw on or even recognize his gifts.

Both may make it to a therapist's office as a fear-based, shame-filled mess. The person who grew up in poverty may see risks of poverty everywhere and make decisions from this inner world, even when there are no risks. He may take jobs he doesn't like just to ensure financial gain; he may become angry if his spouse spends any money. He may deny himself opportunities at happiness because of his fear.

The Driven person beaten into submission may have built his life around staying safe. As a result, he may have avoided the more challenging classes at school because he believes he isn't smart enough for them; he may end up stuck in low-level jobs because he didn't complete his degree. To the world, he may appear to be a plodding clerk or deliveryman, despite the powerful abilities he hasn't realized.

Sometimes a family obligation serves to stifle the Driven's natural gifts and inclinations. Many Drivens go to jobs they hate in the interest of meeting the needs of their families.

A Driven's outer world may not align with their inner world. They may live lives ill-suited to their nature, particularly if they believe they are broken and deserve nothing more, or believe there is nothing better for them. If you are in a leadership role, try to recognize these differences. Matching people to jobs that align with their natural inclinations is a win-win for all stakeholders.

DRIVEN IN ROMANTIC RELATIONSHIPS

As there are benefits for Driven and non-Driven to connect in the workplace, so are there benefits in their personal lives. As in the professional landscape, both Driven and non-Driven romantic partners must be aware of and able to take the perspective of a partner wired differently from themselves.

You might think that two Driven D2/D4s make for an ideal match, and that a Driven married to a non-Driven is sure to be bored. Yet, two Driven D2/D4s are not without their challenges. Drivens who are strong on D2 are impulsive. Two impulsive people, jetting off at a moment's notice, may mean nobody is home to manage the bills, maintain the house, and be responsible to family and friends. Yes, two Drivens may enjoy the same thrill-based vacations and dopamine-seeking spending and partying, but they may also fuel each other's addictions and create total chaos.

Someone needs to be the grown-up. Fortunately, in our service-for-hire society, you can hire someone to do your taxes, ensure that you have groceries in the fridge, cook your meals and have them delivered to your door, and see that your bills are paid on time—you can even hire someone to raise your kids. However, other challenges remain. Remember, Drivens high on D4 may feel that the grass is always greener on the other side. You may be certain your destiny lies in California, while she is sure she belongs in that new job in Hong Kong. Communication and insight from the logical container can alleviate much of these conflicts and help Driven identify a compromise.

What about a Driven and non-Driven union? Clearly, it may be difficult to convince your non-Driven spouse to join you on a skydiving adventure. This is where what you have learned in this book may be extremely helpful. If you convey to your non-Driven spouse that you need this dopamine, and you plan your adventures so that you are taking care of the fun-bucket without ignoring the family-bucket, your spouse is more likely to be content to wait for you at home. It is then possible for both parties to be free of judgment. The Driven aren't guilt-tripped out of their adventures, and the non-Driven know they won't be neglected.

Obviously, tasks of the relationship will fall onto those best suited. The non-Driven partner will ensure that those bills go out on time, the children will be up-to-date on their vaccinations, and there will always be milk in the fridge. The Driven partner will take the risks and face the uncertainties that keep the family safe.

If you look at these challenges through a negative lens, you may talk yourself into being single. If you see the differences through a positive lens, you'll see a world of filled with romantic opportunities. The key is to let the advantages surface and to develop workarounds for those immutable differences that pose conflicts. Again, communication from a logical place with the goal of taking the other's perspective is key. You must remember that you can always view the cup from another side.

Doug goes on frequent adventures to get his dopamine. He grew up hunting and fishing in a D2/D4 household with three Driven brothers. His wife, although up for some adventures, is not Driven for dopamine in the same D2/D4 way. Doug's family jokes about how many "trips of a lifetime" Doug can take in one lifetime.

Early in his marriage, one of Doug's brothers would call with a suggestion for some fun; the Fear of Missing Out (FOMO) would kick in for Doug, and the brothers would plan an impulsive weekend trip. Obviously, Doug had not yet implemented the fun-bucket practice. Doug's wife would feel he was not considering her needs.

What Doug's wife did not understand was that dopamine is a *need* not a *want* for Drivens, and it can create blinding impulsive behaviors if not met. Doug would feel guilty if he went on the unplanned trip, but if he decided not to go, the lack of dopamine could ruin the weekend for both of them. He'd mope around the house wondering how good of a time he was missing, which wasn't fun for him or his wife.

If Doug's need for dopamine was great, he would wait until the last minute to innocently ask what she had planned for the weekend, drawing on the old adage, "It's better to beg for forgiveness than ask for permission." This created lots of tension.

After several years of struggle, Doug implemented the

F-buckets practice, and his wife developed her understanding of what Doug's needs really meant for him. She is now able to support him. She doesn't make him feel guilty about being away from home, as long as the trip is on the calendar with adequate advance notice. The definition of adequate is sometimes still in contention, but it is always discussed, and she understands she is being considered. When he calls from wherever his adventure has taken him, she's happy for him, hoping his adventure has been fulfilling and successful. She accepts his need for dopamine better than he can at times, as Doug still struggles with guilt when he is away. Though he's better at managing it, this guilt still may dampen his excitement.

When we try to suppress what is natural, we may end up channeling those needs in self-sabotaging ways. Many avenues to thrills include devastating risks to get our dopamine. Having scheduled buckets for our dopamine needs ensures that every one of these needs are met; the buckets are also reassuring, not only to us but to our families and friends who know they will not be neglected. Most Driven D2/D4s can good-naturedly tolerate a PTA night, if they know that that weekend they'll be diving with sharks with their buddies. It's easy to let internal experience create a distorted landscape. The key to a successful partnership is appreciation for each other's differences.

HERDS AND PACKS

Our world includes not only our spouses and our families, but our friends too. They constitute a significant part of our lives.

As discussed at length in Chapter 2, humans are dependent on our parents for our complete survival for the longest amount of time of any species on the planet. We are too biologically immature and vulnerable to be left alone, so we need our communities, in addition to our parents, to look after us. We need people.

Human attachment is understood in the context of both a herd and a pack. The differentiating factor between herds and packs is connected to loyalty to the group. At the introduction of danger, herds scatter in all directions. Packs remain together.

From a survival perspective, herds and packs vary in the degree of their dependency on one another. Envision a herd of gazelles clustered together enjoying the sun. Suddenly a cheetah appears. The herd immediately disperses. It is every gazelle for itself. (This phenomenon is common to humans when a highway patrol car enters the freeway. Immediately everyone tenses. If the patrol car singles someone out and pulls them over, the rest of us are immediately relieved that it wasn't us.)

Now envision a pack of wolves. Enter a bear. Unlike the herd that scatters, the pack sticks together and defends one another. They encircle the bear and risk severe bodily injury to save a packmate.

Survival needs explain a great deal about differences in the individual's relationship to the herd or pack. Research supports that individuals who rely heavily on their fight or flight system have a much more difficult time maintaining long-term relationships. As such, Driven may actually be at a disadvantage in making lasting relationships, but as you have seen throughout the book, understanding and perspective-taking greatly impact their experiences.

Drivens are not the gazelles of the world. They are the wolves. As such, they have a pack mentality, willing to do anything necessary to save their friends and loved ones. Doug sees over and over in his practice the fierce sense of loyalty that Driven have towards their families and friends. Time and again a Driven is shocked when this loyalty is not reciprocal.

A Driven will be dumbfounded that his spouse has left him. He would die for her, yet she is able to cut him from her life. Why do Drivens have such fierce loyalty to their friends and even acquaintances, while their non-Driven friends do not come to their defense and do not understand why this has upset them? When attachment is based on the sympathetic branch of the CNS, we may get confusing messages in our gut about what genuine attachment is. We may have a fierce loyalty to our spouse and friends, but do they really return that loyalty? We may blindly give much to others without fully seeing what they would do for us.

The Driven may also go the other way and have few, if any friends. Many Driven have a biased inner world in which they believe others have never done enough for them. If they don't have accurate mirrors in their worlds, they never get the reality check they need. Once on the Mastery Path, they develop greater emotional intelligence and the ability to see the outer world more clearly.

BEYOND EXPECTANCY: USING YOUR MIRRORS

Although Driven D2/D4s may embrace risk and be better able than most to recognize danger, all humans, from a very young age, learn how others can help them when they are scared. This ability is an evolutionary necessity, a key to our survival. Most of us, especially children, use social referencing or mirroring to know when to be afraid. We look at other people we trust to see their reactions. Accurate mirrors highlight the discrepancy between our inner and outer world.

Doug reflects on the way his wife was a mirror for his eldest daughter. When his daughter was two years old and beginning the potty training process, she would run around outside without her diaper. One afternoon, the little girl let out a blood-curdling scream. Her mother, who had been resting inside, sprung up and ran to her daughter—a massive amount of adrenalin coursing through her body. In a near panic, she quickly scanned for injuries or bee stings. Then she saw the poop coming out of the little girl's rear. The scream she heard was not from an injury; it was a scream of complete terror. The child was frightened by the poop (which she was noticing for the first time).

As she ran to her mother, the little girl witnessed the transition of her mother's inner world going from complete terror to relieved calm—the expression on her mom's face changed from wide-eyed fear to smiles and open arms. Seeing that her mother was not frightened, she decided there was no danger from the poop. The mirror neurons in her brain encoded the relief and humor in her mother, and she knew there was no danger. That allowed her inner world to transition from terror to relief. She trusted the reflection sent to her from her mother. Her mother picked her up and hugged her, reassuring her there was nothing to fear.

Experiences like these help us to differentiate the bears from the poop, supporting our accurate assessment of how our inner worlds map to reality. We also learn that when we scream, "Bear!" our pack, in this case, our mother, will come running.

Some Driven report that they really have never trusted anyone, but the importance of reliable mirrors is critical to diminishing the tunnel vision we live with. Who are your trusted mirrors? As Driven D2/D4s, we tend to be hypervigilant for danger, despite our thirst for the thrill it brings. Some D2/D4s will see bears everywhere if they haven't yet set out on the Mastery Path. If other D2/D4s are your mirrors, your mirrors may be biased. Developing the skill to understand others' inner worlds will empower you to find trusted mirrors.

Driven D2/D4s on the Mastery Path can provide you with needed mirrors. We dedicate the next chapter to developing your own wolfpack. Once you have found other like-minded Driven D2/D4s who understand your need for risk, and can multi-think and zoom out from their life map, you will have found the pack support you need. Mirroring can take on a much more effective level of performance. Another Driven will say, "Have you considered this? Have you looked at that? The offramp over there looks like it has a bear, but maybe it's not a bear." The mirroring provided by a loyal pack will offer the feedback you need to discern snakes from ropes.

That said, we also need non-driven people to do reality checks for us. Doug and Randy often hear their clients argue with their spouses or board of directors. "We can't afford *not* to do this," they insist, making a case for spending extra resources for an improvement. The non-driven invariably disagree. Remember, most of the world is satisfied with 3 percent growth, or the current state of the bathroom that does not need remodeling.

If we see outside of our internal experience, seeking to understand why a non-Driven might be seeing something different, we will be able to make sense of the image reflected in that mirror—an image that might prove very informative. To do so, we must put emotional judgment aside and use our natural curiosity to make sense of what we see and hear. It is the cup and handle story; you need to be curious as to what the non-Driven is seeing, just as they need to be curious about your perspective.

· CHAPTER 11 ·

FINDING YOUR WOLFPACK

"As iron sharpens iron, so one person sharpens another."
—PROVERBS 27:17 NIV

The decision to embrace yourself as the Driven D2/D4 you are is a beautiful choice. It is also a scary choice because we're acknowledging that we are different from 90 percent of the population. It's a salient reminder that we may struggle to find people who understand us, think like us, and see the world from our perspective. That said, trying to fit into the herd doesn't work; it forces us to disguise ourselves. We end up feeling like imposters. We belong in a pack.

A pack, as we define it, is a small group of Driven D2/ D4s that support one another. Packs exist in business, in the military, among first responders, on sporting teams, and in a variety of life experiences. The pack supports Driven's needs in many ways. It provides opportunities for camaraderie with others who understand us—who will be valuable mirrors for us—and it gives us a chance to get our needed dopamine in a healthy way.

Many D2/D4s find their packs through mastermind talks, entrepreneurial groups, strategy group sessions, Vistage, and other related professional groups. A mastermind group for marketing or internet entrepreneurs, as an example, provides an opportunity for us to feed off each other's ideas and connect with others Driven D2/D4s.

The SEAL Teams are the epitome of a wolfpack. A typical platoon includes fourteen guys who, over the course of about two years, will work together and develop into a true wolfpack. SEALs come from a very wide spectrum of the population, from the Ivy League-educated to those from street gangs. Their common denominator is that only those with very powerful drives can withstand the pain and torture required to get into this group of extremely high achievers. The SEALs require individual skills and toughness; they also require deep loyalty and investment in the team.

Nearly every movie depicting the SEALs' training showcases the importance of that commitment; six guys in the inflatable, battling together through the oncoming waves, suffering arm in arm in the pitch-black cold surf. SEALs know they have to rely on each other. If one of the team is not pulling his weight, everyone loses. Their members meld together and bond as a pack.

When the selection process begins in BUDs, all the applicants must line up by height and break into groups of six for a boat crew; members need to be a similar height to carry the boat overhead. Everyone must be capable of working together and must be committed to the task. Nothing can interfere, regardless of the situation or problem.

All Drivens have problems, and SEAL Teams are no exception. If a SEAL's problems interfere with his commitment to the pack, he becomes a weak link. The SEALs will not tolerate weakness. These guys know if they make it through the training, they are going to war. They have to trust every member of the platoon to have their back, and when necessary, literally dragging them out of a dangerous situation.

The pack intuitively and quickly senses vulnerability. This process is instinctual. Driven D2/D4 warriors have been like this across the millennia. The Spartans, Romans, and Samurai were well-known for eliminating their weak links.

If a wolf is injured, the pack will gather around him and protect him until he heals. If, however, he is not going to recover, he's going to be their next meal. The pack initially reacts to weakness by bearing fangs at the weakest link. The chief of the platoon or officer-in-charge will address the weakness through a variety of techniques—correction, discipline, or extra work. If the weak link is unfixable, the platoon will naturally begin to push that person out of the pack.

This may sound politically incorrect or even cruel, but it is the law of nature. The safety of the pack depends upon the fact that every pack member depends on every other pack member with his life. The pack will do whatever it takes to get rid of weakness.

Even outside of a military context—in sports or business—Driven D2/D4s do not want a weak link in their organization. The non-Driven see this as harsh, and it may be; but, if you think about it, removing an ill-fitting member may even be a kindness. If you don't belong in the pack, you ultimately aren't going to be happy. Time spent in the pack will be a waste. By identifying weaknesses and remediating or removing its source, we are helping our pack and the pack members who are weak.

Driven warriors, whether in the military or another arena,

know this mindset is critical. Loyalty saves lives. Loyalty means trust.

That said, trust is perhaps one of the more significant challenges for Driven D2/D4s. The Driven tend to be guarded or at least somewhat distrustful of everyone, even their fellow D2/D4s. We have well-honed abilities to detect BS, and a fear-based orientation is clearly a recipe for suspicion. Naturally skeptical, we typically don't give people the benefit of the doubt.

Trust is a misunderstood concept. People tend to think of trust as a feeling; it's not. Trust is not inborn (especially for the Driven). It arises from the outcomes of predictable behavior. Trust can only develop over repeated experiences in which another person has an opportunity to disappoint, but does not. SEAL Teams build trust through experience— through exercises that depend on all members for success.

Despite its incredible value, the pack element is missing from many business environments. Leadership doesn't always recognize the value of a pack. The self-centered direction that guides their decision-making ultimately leaves them vulnerable. They lack the trust required to work as a pack.

Salespeople often keep things to themselves; they don't

help each other in the interest of gaining a competitive edge for themselves. Rather than join the pack, they hunt on their own. Ultimately, this becomes tiring. One person can never accomplish as much as two, two never as much as four. A pack is much more powerful and capable of accomplishing goals than a single person, no matter how hard or smart that person works.

Occasionally, the type of bonds that exist in the SEALs develop in small businesses, especially startups. An extremely tight warrior wolfpack of five or six Driven D2/D4s working together to get a business off the ground can create an ideal situation for an incredible bond. They are creating something revolutionary and everyone is passionate about it. They are all committed to the new organization and to each other.

Growing the business and keeping it successful is the primary responsibility of the pack; they want and need that business to survive. Each pack member must contribute and each pack member is accountable for that contribution.

Businesses can create this commitment in much the same way that SEALs do. Forethought and effort is required. Each member of the pack must have the insight to take the perspectives of the other packmates and the emotional intelligence to be clear about others' intentions. If the pack members are firmly on the Mastery Path, the likelihood of them remaining a unified pack increases dramatically. Additionally, if the members have clearly-defined roles and a mutually stated group purpose, a pack will develop and thrive through the adversity of a new venture.

This kind of life is not for everyone. The kind of commitment required for an entrepreneurial venture exceeds what some initially expected. Even among SEALs, there have been those who've given up their trident because they realized they didn't want to go into combat and were not willing to make the needed sacrifices for their team.

DEVELOPING THE PERSONAL PACK

As Driven, we need accountability in our lives. We also need the opportunity for the kind of camaraderie we find only among those who understand us and have similar needs. Our pack provides for this; it helps us address the friend-bucket.

In his book, *Mastermind Dinners: Build Lifelong Relationships by Connecting Experts, Influencers, and Linchpins,* Jayson Gaignard lays out a formula for developing your own pack. The huge success of the book and demand to be connected to these groups demonstrate how hungry the Driven are to find authentic connection to others like themselves.

Jayson runs a group called Mastermind Talks. He stages it in a way that provides people with opportunities to meet with a few keynote speakers, and then they attend small breakout sessions to bond over specific topics. These smaller groups are ideal for Driven D2/D4s. We can follow and get excited about personally meaningful tangents. This excitement provides the dopamine we need. We meet others like us and carry these connections into the future.

When a non-Driven enters this atmosphere and experiences the excitement and energy of 150 people labeled as ADD/ADHD types, they are typically overwhelmed. Impulsivity, a desire for dopamine along with disposable income tend to create some very interesting relationships and great stories. To a non-Driven, such a group looks like chaos. The pack can become pretty volatile. However, this is where the Driven truly belong. If you're a Driven, you feel at home here with your pack. You feel connected. You feel seen. You feel normal.

You may find that you need to be connected to multiple packs to get your various needs met, but there is a pack (or more) for every Driven. No two packs are the same. Some are strong on testosterone with very rough edges (even among women), while others may be extremely reserved and professional. Regardless of context, a pack of Driven is easy to recognize; you can usually spot them. They almost glow with the laughter and energy they emit. A pack offers much to its members, but it requires a lot, as well. You don't want to start developing a pack until you are stable enough to maintain one.

MAINTAINING YOUR PACK

The health and vitality of the pack depends on several factors. The first requirement of a powerful wolfpack is commitment. Although Driven (once they develop the needed trust) will die for those they care about, they are also impulsive and may say yes to a commitment without thinking through the consequences. All at once, they find themselves over-committed and have no choice but to break their obligations.

Remember, trust is not a feeling. Trust is what results from predictability. If you don't honor your commitments, your reputation may be damaged and people will not invest in you. A pack cannot thrive, let alone develop, without trust. Trust cannot exist if we can't trust our packmates to honor their commitments. Do what you say you will.

When you have your organizational structures—your

F-buckets are in place—you'll maintain your accountability to the people, responsibilities, and obligations in your life. The friends-bucket will help you stay committed to your pack.

Commitment is critical, but perhaps the fastest way to destroy a pack is through selfishness and egocentric thinking. Pack members must put the pack ahead of themselves. Every member must believe that the pack has the individual's best interest in mind, and that what's best for the team is best for the individual.

It takes time to develop trust in the altruistic motivations of our packmates—to internalize they are our trusted mirrors, that they'll help us see through our fear, that they'll give us the needed reality check to know whether we are running from poop or from a bear. It takes time to build the trust needed for the kind of self-disclosure that allows our packmates to be fully supportive and develop a strong pack. Be patient. The trust you need will develop.

Our pack is a home away from home for us, but we are accountable to fulfill our commitment to the pack and its members. A bit of healthy fear ensures we maintain that accountability—we know that the pack might beat up on us a little bit if we don't. This fear encourages us to work hard not to disappoint ourselves, or our pack. We challenge each other. We pull each other out of the depths. Because we need the pack, we rise to its expectations.

The second factor needed for a healthy wolfpack is a wise set of parameters of policies that provide the structure and flexibility needed for decision-making. Everyone in the pack must understand the parameters of the relationship between the pack and its members. While these parameters can (and sometimes must) be negotiated, the pack must have a foundational set of guidelines, essentially a constitution, which is flexible enough to include amendments.

A parameter might be the group's policy on money-lending. Nobody loans money. However, there may be times that this straightforward parameter must be negotiated for the good of the pack. Perhaps one member of the pack is running a business and has a big contract on the table; he needs $10,000 to purchase what he needs to move ahead. This guy has a great history of producing, regardless of the circumstances. The pack may decide in this one case that they can loan this packmate the money because this particular situation might bring the pack financial benefits.

Additionally, the overarching code of the pack is to have each other's backs. If a member needs them, the pack is there for them. Finally, every member of the pack knows that their packmate will absolutely put his entire body, heart, and soul into that investment. Thus, they negotiate the parameter about money-loaning based on their commitment to the pack and to each other.

Confidentiality is also a key parameter. Packs may want a parameter about gossip, or about disclosing pack business to spouses. They may want policies for the addition of new members or guests at get-togethers. These issues need to be discussed before they arise, even if no hard rules are generated. Setting the expectations ahead of time, with the understanding that policies may need to be amended, keeps a pack strong.

The third component of a sustainable wolfpack is engagement. The engagement must be physical. We need a vagal to vagal (heart to heart) connection, and this connection can only occur in the presence of each other. Social media, email, and other forms of electronic communication do one-twentieth of what an actual person-to-person connection will do. Skype allows you to see a face, but nothing is better than the real thing.

A once-a-week meeting is a huge commitment for most Driven D2/D4s, but is well worth any juggling. These frequent get-togethers facilitate the quick development of bonds. Once a month meetings are a minimum if you are committed to making sure your pack is bonded.

Frequent meetings are necessary for pack health; that said, a pack can also be together too much. If a wolfpack is together all the time, friction can develop among the individuals. A group of Driven businessmen, for example, which meets too often will have arguments, usually over insignificant issues that grow large in the eyes of the wolfpack. The same is true for other wolfpacks, even SEALs.

SEALs live, sleep, and eat together for six-to-seven days a week for two straight years. Their bonds are incredibly strong, but the number of physical fights on SEAL Teams speaks to the implications of too much contact and the need for individual space. With that kind of daily close contact, the neural network becomes overtaxed and we get pushed to the edge of our bandwidth. Our fuse gets short and we become easily agitated, getting on each other's nerves.

The antidote for this edginess is a little time apart. Missing the pack is a needed element in the bonding process, as the SEALs demonstrate. Members, on occasion, rotate out for a few weeks to an individual class to learn a specific skill. The degree to which an individual misses his pack, and is missed by the pack, often surprises the Driven warriors.

SEALs are as concerned about their teammates as they are their own families; still, that time apart is important for healthy bonding. When SEALs are away with their families for even just a day during the week, they come back refreshed and feeling significantly better.

Remember also that D2/D4s get bored easily. Being in the same environment with the same people is difficult for us. By changing things up, we can address that potential for boredom. We might meet in different locations. We might, once every few months, have a family barbeque, go shooting, or surfing together. We just need to avoid monotony, in the same way your muscles need some variety at the gym.

The fourth major component of a strong wolfpack is accountability. Accountability is the underlying foundation of the pack—the discipline needed to ensure that the group achieves their goals and objectives. The Mastery Mindset provides personal accountability. It's not a policy or set of guidelines. Rather, it's the promise that all members make to one another and to the pack to honor their obligations and explore their shortcomings. This differs from parameters in that, rather than referring to a policy, it is specific to personal and group accountability as a non-negotiable mindset.

A wolfpack requires a great deal of social, emotional, and

physical commitment from its members. With this investment of time, energy, and emotional focus, we want to be sure we're in the right pack. A continuous assessment of the pack helps accomplish this. Are the pack members committed to one another and to the pack? Do they have sensible parameters? Are the members engaged? If there are problems within the pack, can they be addressed and the needed adjustments made?

In a similar approach to that taken by the SEAL Teams, a healthy wolfpack remediates problems quickly, powerfully, and wisely. Problem-solving requires that members identify and understand the problem(s). Just as important is effective communication across the pack. That communication should include a reminder of the parameters, the expectations, and their commitment.

A pack member who isn't contributing must recognize the consequences of their actions, that they can be thrown out of the pack if they aren't committed. Likewise, the pack must maintain that it is truly better within the pack. Because pack wolves know they are better as a pack, nobody wants to be on their own.

Belonging to a group where we are understood and appreciated is critical for all humans. Being herding creatures is natural for us; that's why we have tribes. In the last hundred years, as neighborhoods have become less connected and the family unit is considerably weaker, having a group is more important than ever before. The wolfpack provides the tribal environment and the vagal connection so important for Driven who may not find it elsewhere.

The importance of this bonded pack is evident in every SEAL. They fear that once they leave the military they will never know that type of camaraderie again. This camaraderie goes beyond what civilians understand; it is so valuable and powerful that it affects the rest of their lives. We want it. We crave it.

What SEALs (and other Driven) need to recognize is that we can have the same level of camaraderie in other wolfpacks. We just have to understand that this camaraderie will only occur with other Driven D2/D4s. We can make the same type of commitment to other wolfpacks that we made to our SEAL team buddies. Randy makes that same commitment to whatever pack he joins.

The Bible tells us, "As iron sharpens iron, so one person sharpens another." This is what we do in our packs and what the pack does for us. According to Rev. J. Benson, this sharpening "quickens his ingenuity, enlivens his affections, strengthens his judgment...and makes him, in all respects, a better man."

· CHAPTER 12 ·

ACHIEVING MASTERY?

"The happiness of a man in this life does not consist in the absence, but in the mastery of his passions."

—ALFRED LORD TENNYSON

There is an old riddle that asks, "If there are three frogs on a log, and one makes the decision to jump off, how many frogs are left?" The answer is three. A decision without action means nothing. The frog can decide all he wants, but if he doesn't jump, he remains on the log.

We can decide to quit smoking, eat healthier, go to the gym, or spend more time with our families. That doesn't mean this will happen.

Commitment is important, but it's critical to recognize

that it takes time to execute our decisions, especially those that push us outside of our bandwidth. It takes time to expand that bandwidth so these decisions are comfortable for us. We don't learn trigonometry or read the world's greatest books in an hour. Learning is a slow and gentle process. It is lifelong and never-ending.

The Mastery Path is about not making big decisions or big changes. It's the micro-commitments and the micro-adjustments we make that constitute this constant state of learning. A small change does not trigger resistance in our elephant; it allows us to slowly expand our bandwidth.

If we appreciate and are grateful for this progress, if we celebrate the small steps, we can enjoy the reinforcing feelings of satisfaction. We don't lose heart; we don't give up. We don't focus on a specific point in the distance because we're not interested in a specific location on the path, only the path itself. The Mastery Path is perpetual. There is no finish line. We keep learning.

Along the Mastery Path, we choose from the ten thousand behaviors available to use throughout the day. We approach every decision with curiosity, from the opportunity of doing something different and the possibility that our action is in perfect alignment with our life's purpose and intention. Of course, perfect alignment is never possible, but we can get better and better.

The development of any new skill includes plateaus. The skills we learn on our Mastery Path are no exception. We often get stagnant as we reach a plateau, tempted to think, "This isn't working." It is at these plateaus we must recognize the incredible strength in the micro-process of acquiring a new skill. We grow in tiny increments. Mysteriously, the tiny increments come together in a new way, and we have new insight and a new skill. We move to the next plateau.

You must appreciate these increments as steps along the path, learn to love the plateaus, and not be fixated on the next level. Fixating on a particular point on the infinite number line returns you to a mindset of "if only" thinking, and the erroneous and toxic belief that this point is going to make everything perfect. We are back hoping to finish climbing this pole so we can get to the next. However, there is no pole—there never was, and never will be.

The learning process itself should be our focus. There is incredible, often-unexpected value in the learning experience and in the opportunity to make those very small adjustments that move us along the path. Appreciate this process; enjoy the feeling of making those micro-adjustments. True Mastery is never achieved; it is only practiced.

The key to developing Mastery is to be able to ask, *"What am I doing?"* without any shame. Whether you are parenting or being a spouse, or starting a business, there is no place for judgment—only curiosity.

As a parent, you ask yourself, "What is my intention in parenting?" We must drop the judgment of attempting to know what a good parent is; rather, we rest in the intention that we are attempting to provide a healthy atmosphere for our kids and raise morally sound, competent, independent, and loving people. If your son asks for a popsicle an hour before dinner, you might tell him, "No." He might get angry and throw a temper tantrum, but you're able to step back and know you're doing what's best for your family and for you. You can emotionally rest in your loving intention. You don't judge, you don't react to a fear-based ping, even if his whining sends waves of frustration and doubt through your body. Rest in your heart knowing this is what's best. You can then set clear boundaries and consequences to address his whining without letting the impulse to scold drive your behavior. We reflect on how parenting can always be improved to match your intention. As your children develop, your style will need to adjust, but your intention may not deviate over their lifetime.

Fear and self-judgment no longer guide your behavior, but rather, your constant state of curiosity helps improve your parenting to meet the new demands of the circumstance.

This isn't about playing the violin without any mistakes. If you set those expectations, you are back to judging and beating yourself up. You become afraid to play the violin, afraid to hit that tennis ball, and afraid to parent your kid. You miss so much in life. Instead of letting fear drive your actions, simply live the full intention of being a father, mother, or student—always attempting to be better, always growing.

KNOWING YOUR PURPOSE: USING YOUR GIFTS FOR GOOD, NOT EVIL

As a Driven, you can use the gifts you once saw as a problem as a wonderful opportunity. These gifts can help you change the world. That said, we want to be sure we're using these gifts for good. Sometimes the different perspectives of the Driven and the non-Driven make it difficult for those without our genetics to understand that our hearts are in the right place. It's so important that we communicate clearly and approach situations from a place of curiosity. The question "why" can go a long way in keeping relationships healthy and strong.

There's an old AA saying that, "You have to be messed

up and broken to become a member, and any time you think you're fixed, you're not." Being in that evolutionary place, among others, with the understanding that you are always improving yourself becomes very infectious.

Accountability is not judgment of the self or others. It's this gentle tug back to the path. It's that calmness within yourself and others that is critical. It's curiosity without judgment of shame. Accountability doesn't mean, "I'm on the hook for the result." It means, "You're on the hook for improving yourself."

How do you do this? You do this by acknowledging your gifts. Seek out other Driven D2/D4s to sharpen those gifts. When you approach people who are also on this path, help them. Tell them, "Dude, come on back. Come between the guardrails. You're way out in la-la land. What are you doing? You're better than this."

You don't judge them. You don't shame them. Helping others this way helps you to help yourself. It supports that vital non-judgmental accountability.

Daniel Amen, one of the foremost brain researchers in ADD and ADHD, terms D2/D4s as sheepdogs and non-Driven as sheep. According to Amen, 95 percent of the population are sheep. Sheepdogs protect the sheep from danger. Look at any group of firefighters, police, military, or first responders, and you'll see that most of these people are D2/D4s protecting the sheep.

When you protect someone, you also run the risk of antagonizing him or her. Non-Driven may not recognize you have their best interests at heart. Some even accuse you of being wolves out to eat them as sheep. They are positive that you're trying to hurt them.

Not everyone sees the greater good in an action. Most parents have heard their children rant at them, calling them hateful and unfair. A non-Driven adult may accuse us in much the same way. "You're a bad friend. I don't ever want to talk to you again!"

D2/D4s that are good, morally motivated people can still be seen as evil. How we appear to others is a function of the communication barriers between the Driven and non-Driven and the challenges related to perspective-taking. Those without our gifts do not always understand our good intentions, and they may react accordingly.

We must guard against the feelings of shame coming from those who don't understand us. We must grab the opportunity to share our purpose. Unfortunately, we won't always get a chance to explain our purpose (something which, as you have learned, can make a Driven absolutely crazy). However, even if others don't understand our true intentions, we need to remember if our purpose and intentions were good, then—even if our intentions weren't transparent and the outcome wasn't what we had hoped—we haven't used our gifts for evil.

It's important to note that we do have the ability to be very manipulative; we can become chameleons and hide our true intentions (which for some of us are not in the interest of bringing good). There are Driven D2/D4s who focus on making money and using their gifts for immediate satisfaction. They want their dopamine and don't consider the impact of their actions, or they do consider the impact but choose not to care. In that, we can be evil. Even if our actions aren't driven by selfishness, as Driven D2/D4s, we can be impulsive. Even if we didn't intend to hurt others, this impulsivity, while not necessarily evil, can be very hurtful.

If, however, we are on the Mastery Path with a sense of purpose, we are safeguarded against using our powerful gifts for the wrong purpose. We have a plan for catching our impulses so we can choose our behaviors.

Be clear that you're not evil. Be clear that you are doing what you do for a greater good. When other people judge you, you will not be driven to prove anything. You will be free just to be.

As you step onto the Mastery Path, you won't be driven by fear. There is no pole to climb, so you need not be afraid you won't reach the top. There is no reason to wear a disguise, no reason to hide yourself; you're okay.

You have no need to self-sabotage. You don't need to change the outer world to reflect your inner world; there is just the one world. You may feel like you aren't good enough, but this is your normal. You're a Driven. You're wired to feel things aren't right and aren't safe; it's your gift to humanity. It is the reason mankind has survived. There's no place where you'll feel safe because you're already safe. There's no special thing you must do to be okay, because you're already okay, right now.

ABUNDANCE, GRATITUDE, AND GRACE

Our logical brain is something of a ledger for our lives. As Driven D2/D4s, it was once a scoreboard for our failures. Shame would then be justified in the emotional brain and we suffered. This shame and self-hatred filled our bodies with a toxic soup of stress hormones and adrenaline. As you've learned, this never has to be lived again.

The logical brain can also be used as a ledger for our abundance. It reminds us, "Yes, I can be a better parent, but my children are doing fairly well. Yes, I can be a better boss, but my employees seem happy." The logical brain allows us to take stock of where we're strong and reminds us where we can improve. The emotional brain can then feel gratitude for all that we have in our life. Gratitude blossoms when we learn to feel grateful for all those small advantages and benefits we often disregard. Take stock in these things often.

When we know gratitude, we begin to feel grace. Grace is a physical shift in the body. It's an *unearned* peace and contentment and for the Driven which we don't believe we've fully earned. This is critical to remember. To drop this gratitude into the body, feel it internally, and fully embody grace is a challenge for the Driven.

Remember, resistance is simply the inability to step into the future from a curious and open mind. People resist going to the gym because they can't experience what good health feels like—they have an underlying fear that they don't really deserve it. They can't envision it. All they know is they've been going to the gym for two months and they aren't seeing progress. Their workouts hurt and they aren't fun. These people aren't thinking in terms of small adjustments; they have a goal (I want to lose thirty pounds) and when this doesn't happen, they feel like they have failed. In the face of what they perceive as failure, they sabotage further efforts. They no longer go to the gym, which provides them the validation they seek in the outer world that confirms the inner world sense of failure. They are climbing the pole of success, rather than knowing that in grace they can feel the appreciation for just walking through the door of the gym.

If, however, they conceptualize their gym visits as small adjustments, and they decide to go once a week in January, twice a week in February, and three times a week in March, they have redirected the goal. They no longer focus on losing thirty pounds, but are grateful for the small changes toward better fitness. Going to the gym becomes an exercise in building a grace-filled life. They're not trying to earn the good feeling that comes from going to the gym or having a fit body. They feel good about going and *being* at the gym.

They feel those micro-shifts happen in their body. They are grateful for going to the gym, and grateful for thirty minutes on the treadmill when they used to only be able to do twenty minutes. As they begin to embody these positive emotions, they experience grace. They overcome the resistance in their body. Grace allows good feelings to permeate the body. It's the feeling of safety and contentment that is grounded in *what they are being*. They don't weigh themselves anymore. Their perspective has shifted. It's the infinite journey to *being* healthier. Yes, during the holidays, they may gain a few pounds, as the family-bucket takes a priority over their time at the gym, but they don't judge. They don't fear. They have the accountability and grace and can gently return to the gym when time allows.

This type of thinking and being is a true shift in the reward system of the Driven brain. Grace allows us to continue forever. There is no place to get to and no finish line. This is ideal for a Driven because we're never satisfied. But a journey with no finish line means there is no way to fail and no way for sabotage. There is only gratefulness for the progress we make and the grace to continue this process throughout our lives.

The Mastery Path allows a life engaged in change and the visualization of true possibility. Whether you are an entrepreneur, a teacher, a firefighter, a student, a parent—what you're trying to learn, what you want is bigger than you. But to achieve it, you must begin with yourself. Through meditation and grace, we gain the insight to be able to stand back and zoom out without judgment, just live. When you experience *self* as whole and complete, always striving to be better, your bigger purpose will naturally become clear.

This bigger purpose applies in everything we do—from parenting, to being a good friend, to our careers. A stable CNS empowers us with the ability to not only see, but also feel where we want to go. When our nervous system is stable, we can ask, "How does it feel be a salesperson in a room full of people, completely prepared, with the purpose of helping them? What am I really trying to do? I'm not there to make money. I am there to convey this great message." Grace allows this feeling to be fully embodied and carried into reality.

You can visualize by closing your eyes and imagining yourself standing in front of your audience. Very quickly, your hyperfrontal lobe will start to multi-think about all of the negative scenarios. However, if you visualize what it'll be like to have great slides for your presentation, to see the engaged faces of the audience, and most importantly, the way this would feel in your body, you'll know what it means to be embodied with these sensations, and you'll carry them into reality.

Knowing the feelings in our bodies of not quitting, of dealing with a screaming child, of delivering a critical presentation, lets us drop the self-centered focus, preparing us for a greater purpose. We experience congruence between all three minds, and as they blend into one, we ultimately experience our larger *self* in everything we do.

This deeper truth doesn't come from a poster board with pictures of big houses, boats, and cars that we look at and tell ourselves, "One day, when I get that, I'm going to be okay." This truth doesn't originate from a place of fear. Rather, we develop the ability to manifest in our body the feeling of having what we want. We *feel* that achievement before it happens. With grace, we're freed from questioning whether we deserve it or not. We know how it feels to be a great father, teacher, spouse, or writer. We can tolerate whatever challenges come with this, because we know what it feels like, and we know why we do what we do.

You have no need to self-sabotage. You're okay. You strive to be better because better has no finish line. You don't need to change the outer world to reflect your inner world; there is just the one world.

You're a Driven. Remember, when you experience *self* as whole, always striving to be better, your bigger purpose will naturally become clear.

ABOUT THE AUTHORS

Doug and Randy's paths crossed at the shooting range. Doug, a clinical psychologist, was the student; Randy, a former Navy SEAL and entrepreneur, the teacher. As they got to know each other, they had a lot in common and this led to a close friendship. Both worked closely with Driven D2/D4s—Doug in his practice and Randy through his military experiences.

Doug believed the mindfulness required by long-range shooting and meditation could be applied to help people gain control of their drive. Together, they dug into this idea and examined martial arts and meditation practices in different parts of the world. They realized that throughout history, there have been cultures, like the Japanese warriors, that have intuitively figured out the connections between brain and body, and the enormous control that alignment can bring. Science is now recognizing these connections and the value of that alignment.

Their combined interests and talents led them to develop a simple and powerful form of mindfulness training designed specifically for D2/D4s. Borrowing heavily from the Rinzai Ji type of Japanese Zen, modern bio-hacking, and fMRI research, Zazen meditation perfectly maps to the needs of the highly Driven. Zazen meditation is practical, works quickly (Driven D2/D4s are not patient and want to see results right away), and requires that one draw on all their senses, keeping their eyes open. This is important for D2/D4s. They are visually oriented and wired not to let their guard down. Zazen meditation is not used to shut anything out, run from anything, escape, transcend reality, or even relax. The purpose of Zazen meditation is to connect with the present moment. This is a natural inclination for D2/D4s who must be alert to everything in their world all at once.

Doug and Randy help their clients discover that they are all right. Rather than thinking of all the things they must accomplish before they can be "okay," these Driven are able to shift their perspective. They see that right now they are fine, but they can always be better. This resonates with D2/D4s; they are always driven to be better.

Both Doug and Randy have firsthand experience living with the challenges inherent in a Driven's genetics.

Before Doug learned to manage his gift, he was a high school dropout living in a car. By the age of eighteen, he was living on the streets and was already a recovering alcoholic. Sometime after his eighteenth birthday, he figured out that living this way was not what he wanted. He decided to do something different with his life. That decision led to some inner questioning, and then to his wondering, "What's wrong with me?" But nothing was wrong with him. Doug's strong Driven genetics were a mismatch for a farmer's world. Once he figured out how to direct them, these same genetics provided a resilience and perseverance that earned him two PhDs.

Learning to harness Driven gifts is not easy, especially for a population that naturally views the world with skepticism. Yet this skepticism, this natural curiosity and questioning, provides the tools that ultimately set them on the path to Mastery.

47102047R00190

Made in the USA
Middletown, DE
16 August 2017